Middle Eastern Lectures

Number Two

1997

The Moshe Dayan Center for Middle Eastern and African Studies seeks to contribute by research, documentation, and publication to the study and understanding of the modern history and current affairs of the Middle East and Africa. The Center is part of the Aranne School of History and the Lester and Sally Entin Faculty of Humanities at Tel Aviv University.

Middle Eastern Lectures is a biennial publication of the Moshe Dayan Center. It serves to disseminate outstanding lectures delivered by visitors to the Center. Manuscript submissions are not solicited.

Middle Eastern Lectures is published by Tel Aviv University. It is distributed worldwide by Syracuse University Press, 1600 Jamesville Avenue, Syracuse, NY 13244-5160; and in Israel by the Publications Department, the Moshe Dayan Center for Middle Eastern and African Studies, Tel Aviv University, Ramat Aviv 69978. Other recent and forthcoming Center publications are listed at the back of this issue.

This issue has been edited by Martin Kramer.

Middle Eastern Lectures
Number Two
1997

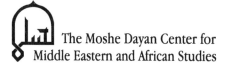

The Moshe Dayan Center for
Middle Eastern and African Studies

Tel Aviv University

Cover illustration: *Le Marchand de tapis au Caire* (The Carpet Merchant), by Jean-Léon Gérôme, *c.* 1887, The Minneapolis Institute of Arts

ISBN 965-224-023-0

CONTENTS

Editor's Note

The painting by Jean-Léon Gérôme that graces the cover of this issue is entitled *The Carpet Merchant*. It evokes an economic transaction among Muslims at the last moment in history when the Muslim world could claim a measure of economic independence. But by the time Gérôme painted this stunning variation on a favorite Orientalist theme, the carpets displayed here most likely would have been destined for salons in Europe and America. A traditional art, itself the very epitome of self-reliance, had become an industry geared to the tastes of the West.

This issue of *Middle Eastern Lectures* opens with two lectures on Muslim dreams of restored economic independence. Charles Tripp considers the contemporary Muslim critique of capitalism, Timur Kuran surveys the utopian ideas of Islamic economics. Judith Miller complements this discussion with a firsthand report on three Islamists who would break the spell of the West.

Politics can also be a dismal science. P.J. Vatikiotis compares the autocracy of monarchies and republics in the Middle East, and finds depressing similarities. Yezid Sayigh argues that even the end of the cold war and an Arab-Israeli peace cannot resolve the deeper crisis that besets the Arab world. Bernard Lewis dwells on a period of greater confidence, reflecting on traditional Muslim historiography.

The two concluding lectures treat the cultural interaction of Muslims and Jews. Norman A. Stillman finds the common threads of a Judeo-Islamic civilization, and Dan V. Segre appreciates a Jewish scholar, Giorgio Levi Della Vida, who found inspiration in all three monotheisms.

Since the last publication of *Middle Eastern Lectures*, my colleague Asher Susser has stepped down from the directorship of the Moshe Dayan Center. The initiative for this series belonged to him, and I will always be grateful for his vision and persistence in lifting our project off the ground.

Martin Kramer

"The Enemy Within": Islamic Responses to Capitalism in the Middle East

by Charles Tripp

In this lecture, I will examine various attempts in the Middle East over the past fifty years to devise distinctively Islamic responses to capitalism. The responses under scrutiny here are intellectual. The writers who formulated them sought to understand the nature as well as the power of capitalism. But they were also strategic, intended to enable Muslims to resist the acknowledged seductions of the capitalist mode of production, and to construct an order of equal efficacy and power, resting on Islamic ideals. They sought to transform and strengthen Islamic societies, while preserving a distinctively Islamic character for the principal forms of economic activity.

The interest of capitalism for social scientists — as for its Islamic critics — lies in the fact that it is associated with much more than the narrowly defined economic techniques or processes that lie at the heart of the capitalist creation of wealth. Capitalism expresses and engenders distinctive forms of political power and particular hierarchies. This can be seen, for example, in the class divisions at the heart of capitalist enterprise. It can also be seen in the laws which guarantee the rights of owners to dispose of their property as they see fit, and to exclude others from it.

The acceptance or legitimation of this political order is connected to beliefs which shape the economic and political institutions congenial to a capitalist society. Most obvious, in terms of the historical development of capitalism, have been attitudes towards the pursuit of profit. Avarice and the relentless desire by individuals to accumulate capital through profit were no longer seen as a disruptive passion, but rather as a steadying "interest." This rational drive would produce the growth that would, in theory, benefit all.

These attitudes rested on an ethic both secular and individualist. They assumed society to be made up of individuals whose wants and needs, when taken together, constituted the sum of human happiness. The endless drive for acquisition would lead towards this ever-extendable goal. The secular aspect of this worldly striving derived from the belief that such happiness was attainable through the satisfaction of material wants, without invoking divine sanction or telos as justification.

The commercialization of life which this implies draws more and more areas of life into the capitalist circuit, driven by competition for profits. The process is sanctioned by the tendency to see everything, including ideas, as a commodity with a capacity for yielding profit. These various themes will be found in different combinations in different places, with varying emphasis now on one aspect, now on another. All, however, will be made more plausible and authoritative by the very success of the capitalist enterprise.

Those drawn into a global economy dominated by capitalist forces and values faced challenges of two kinds. First, how could they preserve existing values and identities in the face of the remorseless power of the states, enterprises, organizations and systems of ideas which stood at the forefront of European capitalist and imperialist expansion? On a social, political and intellectual level, the economic power of capitalism had severely disruptive effects. Old technologies and ways of life were rapidly made redundant, undermining the raison d'être of existing communities and creating new ones around productive enterprises geared to capitalist production. This created new hierarchies and elites, espousing values and achieving success by the new criteria that came to dominate the economic systems of the capitalist West.

Second, there was the question of the intellectual challenge associated with these processes. Sociological, economic and political discourses demanded new vocabularies to render intelligible the new categories and processes. Capitalism and its associated systems of thought involved new assumptions, terms and claims which were to transform the ways people thought about their own societies.

The breathtaking radicalism of the assumptions about human nature, society and the place of man in the order of things, together with the often dehumanizing effects of industrial capitalism, have provoked a variety of responses. In the heart of industrial capitalism's emergence, the European continent, this has ranged from the secular critique of capitalism by the utopian socialists and Marx, to the equally vehement moral outrage expressed by the Christian socialists and, in a rather different way, by the Roman Catholic Church.[1] Some thought that the logic

10

of capitalist enterprise suppressed human potential. Others feared that the power and ubiquity of capitalism would destroy the foundations of an ethical universe.

The responses which emerged in the Islamic world to the advent of industrial capitalism should be viewed in this context. There are striking parallels with the responses that emerged in Europe in a quite different cultural idiom. As elsewhere, people could not remain unaffected by this great transformation. Capitalist enterprise extended its commercial logic to the Middle East, along with new technologies, systems of organization, disciplines and seductions, class stratification, political structures and ideologies. It caught people up in its system, subjecting them to forces over which they had no control and impelling them towards destinations not of their own choosing.

The emerging new world of capitalism created a disciplinary order of immense social power. For some, this was a mesmerizing opportunity, promising to release the untapped potential of the Middle East which, if harnessed to a proper ethical end, might yet be put to the service of a greater ideal. For others, the very process itself held grave dangers for the ethical order of Islam, threatening to destroy it whilst holding out the enticing possibility of strengthening it. These are the twin poles of fascination and repulsion that mark the writings of those who have tried to construct a distinctively Islamic response to capitalism. General Islamic discourse and the writings of particular individuals are drawn taut between them.

The Culture of Capitalism

Most of the writers who have articulated self-consciously Islamic responses to capitalism acknowledge its power to attract human beings, to induce them to the exclusive pursuit of advantages in this world, and to shape their relations to each other and to God. The concern of these writers has therefore been to redirect human energies in order to ensure that all economic transactions are restrained by the ethical system of Islam — to ensure, in other words, that people are continually reminded of their obligations to God, and do not forget the relative insignificance of transactions in this world when measured against the relationship with God in the next.

There seems to have been general agreement that Western capitalism had given a new and dangerous impetus to a force in human nature which the Islamic revelation was specifically designed to keep in check — hence the Egyptian thinker Muhammad al-Ghazzali's remark (made in the 1950s) that "Communism is the enemy standing at the gates, and capitalism is the enemy within."[2] This phrase, which I have incorporated in the title of this lecture, can be read on three levels.

The first, clearly intended by Ghazzali, was the sense in which capitalism appealed to aspects of human nature which the Islamic revelation came to restrain. The pursuit of profit free of all ethical restraint encouraged human beings to lose sight of the moral order ordained by God and to behave egotistically. Second, Ghazzali referred to the institutions of post-colonial Middle Eastern societies. Thus, capitalist forms, procedures and institutions had insinuated themselves into the societies in which Muslims lived, and those who wished to see the establishment of an authentically Islamic order needed some strategy to deal with the "enemy within."

However, there is a third level of meaning, probably ignored by Ghazzali, but which I shall argue colors his responses and those of the other self-consciously Islamic authors. The argumentation of those who tried to devise an Islamic response to capitalism was heavily influenced by the values of the very system they themselves criticized. In other words, the "logic" of capitalism, or of the ideological presuppositions associated with its emergence and development, unmistakably informs the arguments of the Islamic writers.

As with others who have criticized the disruptive and morally repugnant aspects of capitalism, Islamic critics of capitalism have seized upon certain of its features which they have regarded as potentially destructive of Islamic values. These features could be said to comprise both the institutions of a fully developed capitalist order, and the justifying rationales underlying them — or, in an idealist view, the ideology that has given rise to them. The list and the emphasis vary from writer to writer, but there seems to be general agreement about the actually or potentially dangerous effects of four clusters of features. Analytically, it is necessary to separate them, but in fact and certainly in the writings of the Islamic authors, they are treated as an interconnected whole. Running through their critique is the reiterated claim that all of these aspects are present in all societies, but that under the "culture of capitalism" they have been allowed to flourish without moral restraint.

The most obvious symptom of capitalism is the emergence of self-confident individualism as a justification for economic behavior. This is equated with a moral egotism which runs counter to Islamic values (and indeed to those of most religious systems). In the views of most of the writers, egotism has been encouraged by capitalism to such an extent that it has ruptured social harmony, eroding bonds of cohesion and creating a universe of atomized individuals whose sole measure of value is material acquisition.

This, in turn, has made the utilitarian calculus the measure of all things, revolving around the hedonistic individual. Nor can this easily be separated from the secular impulse to disenchant the world of things and of human relations. Under such an uncompromisingly worldly view, things merely have a use value. They become commodities whose value can be quantified through that foremost agent of disenchantment: money. The power of money to "disembed" objects and indeed human relationships from their ethical context had always been suspect in the eyes of Islamic thinkers.[3] Now they feared that the dominant economic institutions of capitalism were geared precisely towards this end, encouraging the commodification of all things in the service of profit.

In such a culture, money and the institution of private property are seen as socially destructive. In the view of most of the Islamic writers, the institutions themselves are not to blame. The danger lies instead in the purpose to which they have been put, and to the fact that capitalism lifts any restraint upon their use in the pursuit of individual profit. These institutions become temples of individualism, restricting people's view of the community and of the divine order. It is in this context that the majority of these writers look upon the institution of interest, equated by most of them with *riba*. Not only is *riba* specifically forbidden in the Qur'an, but interest is seen as monetary profit completely divorced from social or ethical restraint, giving it a dangerous power. The prohibitions on *riba*, therefore, and the various devices constructed to permit the full enjoyment of property within the framework of an Islamic value system, seek to oblige money and private property to serve an Islamic ideal.

The difficulty of achieving this under a dominant capitalist system leads these writers to pay some attention to a fourth aspect of capitalism: the market. Again, all of them agree that this is a necessary institution, since it is the site of the exchange of information, goods and services. However, their fear is that under capitalism, it has become the arena for a ruthless competition unrestrained by ethical scruples. As such, it has become the institutional framework for the realization of utilitarian values, governed by the measure of money. The market can have a powerful and productive effect, generating new technologies that open up new avenues for profit. Potentially, however, it is also the battlefield of class conflict and social war.

They acknowledge the power of all these features of capitalism in human life, but argue that they must be brought under a system of effective moral restraint, in the service of the community and founded upon Islamic law, the *shari'a*. This corresponds with Ghazzali's first meaning of "the enemy within." Furthermore, capitalism's link with Western imperialism has shaped their response. This has led some to utopian ideas about the possible autonomy or autarchy of their own societies, and visions of cutting links of dependency to a world economic order dominated by capitalist institutions and values. This corresponds to Ghazzali's second meaning of "the enemy within."

Beyond that, however, ambiguity begins to cloud their writings. It is here that I would argue that the third meaning of "the enemy within" comes into play. Those, including Ghazzali himself at the time, who sought to counteract the socially disintegrating effects of capitalism by imaginatively reconstructing an ideal Islamic society, found that they were obliged to think in terms of "society" and of "social utility," paradoxically drawing them closer to a utilitarian perspective, albeit of a broadly socialist variety. The same applies to those who have tried to invent a distinctively "Islamic economics," resting on the imaginative construct of a *homo Islamicus*. Here, too, the imaginative project is informed by an individualist and utilitarian logic which owes its origins to the very discourses of capitalist economics it seeks to counter.

Saving Islam, Saving Society

As illustrations, let us look at two aspects of the Islamic response to capitalism. Both trace their intellectual origins to individuals such as Afghani and Abduh, who wrote extensively about what they then called the "social problem." This already involved a significant transition from thinking about the *umma*, or community of the faithful, to the more general category of *al-mujtama'*, society or the collection of individuals. The terminological shift presaged the debate about the effects of capitalism in the twentieth century. Both aspects can be best traced through the works of two broad groups of authors: those primarily concerned with social justice and solidarity, and those preoccupied with societal development and economic growth.

To the first group belong writers such as Abd al-Qadir Awda, Sayyid Qutb, Bahi al-Khuli, Muhammad al-Bahi and many of those associated with the Muslim Brotherhood in Egypt, as well as Mustafa al-Siba'i in Syria.[4] These men were alarmed by the effects of capitalism upon the Islamic identities of their societies. In particular, they were concerned about the relationship between private property and social cohesion.

For them, capitalism posed a danger because it freed men from any sense of the obligations under which they held property. Following the orthodox Islamic view, they argued that God was the sole owner of all creation and had entrusted man with the material world that he might profit from its use. This gave rise to the institution of property from which man might legitimately profit, as long as he obeyed the *shari'a* in his property transactions. In their view, this gave profit much wider significance than it enjoyed in the narrowly material accounting of capitalism.

In this account of property, however, they recognized the existence of a certain tension. Property, despite its divine origins and the conditions of the trust, was clearly a product of man's impulse to exploit and accumulate. These potentially dangerous aspects of property required men to be constantly reminded of their status as trustees of God's creation. This had been the very purpose of the definitive revelation of the Prophet Muhammad, leading to the establishment of the short-lived but perfect Islamic order. In their writings, the harmony of the early Islamic community derived in part from the ways in which property was managed and disposed. Managed in this way, property could be an instrument of social cohesion. Individual benefit equated with the benefit of the community, as long as the trustee abided by the conditions of the trust, which included meeting social as well as individual needs.

In all of these writings, the categories "society" and "individual" are used with increasing frequency, a dualism that echoes more secular debates. For instance, writers assumed that it would always be possible to define individual and social needs, and their respective claims to resources. Yet they recognized that in practice, scripture offered little guidance on how to do this. They also recognized that there might be a conflict between the duty to profit and the duty to assist the materially deprived.

Some of these writers also reflected upon the possibility that the striving of the individual to renounce need might conflict with the idea that individual needs collectively formed the sum of social needs. This debate echoed Weber's famous characterization of the capitalist as an "inner worldly ascetic." Furthermore, there were those who argued that in an Islamic society, Muslims need property to realize their ethical potential, through payment of *zakat* and through other acts of communal solidarity.

In the end, most of these authors elevated "social need" above all else. That which enhanced social solidarity was deemed obligatory. The promotion of social harmony was admitted as the only justification for property. This, they claimed, was God's purpose in creating the conditions of trusteeship under which people might enjoy the use of property. In this argument, collective claims on property embody the "rights of God" vis-à-vis property — that is, the conditions God expects will be fulfilled in human transactions involving property. These conditions of trusteeship thus become linked to two criteria of social utility which inform the subsequent debate about property in capitalist and Islamic systems. The first criterion is the reinforcement of the bonds of social solidarity and the second revolves around largely utilitarian considerations of public welfare.

According to the works of these writers, these criteria are to be discovered by a close reading not simply of the *nass* (text) of the holy scripture, but also of the *nass* of society itself. The rationally discovered needs of society provide the social "text" of validation. Some of these writers justified this through reference to methodologies used by Muslim jurists to find answers for questions about which the text of the scripture itself seems silent. Thus, *al-masalih al-mursala*, "benefits not specified in the scripture," justified the invocation of public welfare to determine the correct course of action. Equally, the invocation of *sadd al-dhara'i'*, "blocking of the means," was used to underpin judgments on procedures which, even if they appeared lawful in the *shari'a*, are thought to have socially harmful effects. Similarly, these writers used examples from the life of the Prophet or the Rashidun Caliphs to prove that decisions about the proper conduct of Muslims could legitimately be based upon the notion of the public interest.

The significance of these developments in the reasoned responses to capitalism is threefold. First, they indicate that capitalism was being indicted increasingly for its harmful *social* effects: anomie, alienation, the breakdown of community and social solidarity, the atomization of the individual and inequalities. This implied universal, rather than distinctively Islamic notions of society, social good and social cohesion. Second, they suggested that capitalism confronted the Islamic world with unprecedented problems that could not be addressed through "conventional" readings of Islamic obligation derived from the texts of the scripture. Third, they introduced utilitarian preoccupations into interpretations of Islamic obligation. The contingency of reason and the utilitarian calculus increasingly informed the readings of Islamic obligation derived from the texts. Thus, in the attempt to respond to capitalism from an Islamic perspective, these writers willy-nilly became caught up in the terms and categories of the secular critique of capitalism — a critique that was, of course, based on many of the assumptions and values that underpinned the "culture of capitalism" itself. Perhaps for this very reason, Sayyid Qutb eventually turned his back on this whole approach. For him, the categories of "society" and "social needs," even "reason" itself, had to be repudiated, and faith alone invoked, if the integrity of Islam was to be preserved.[5]

An Islamic Economy

Similar preoccupations and problems have marked the writings of the second group defined above: those who have been concerned above all with the growth strategies and development potential of Islamic societies. Taking their inspiration largely from the seminal work of Muhammad Baqir al-Sadr in Iraq, this group includes people such as Ahmad al-Najjar, Abd al-Hamid Abu Sulayman, Muhammad Saqr, Mahmud Ansari, as well as numerous authors from South and Southeast Asia.[6] These thinkers and writers are associated with attempts both to imagine an "Islamic economy," and to give it first expression through Islamic banks.

The actual experience of these attempts will not detain us here, interesting though they may be. Rather, my intention is to ask how these attempts to conjure up an economic system and institutions to rival the power of capitalism succumbed to capitalism's own logic. Just as those who were preoccupied with social solidarity and social justice wound up being labelled "Islamic socialists," so too the Islamic economists and bankers have been unable to escape the consequences of seeking to counter capitalism on its own terrain.

One of the main rationales given for an "Islamic economics" was that economic programs and developmental schemes elaborated in the West were inappropriate to Islamic society. This inappropriateness was assessed very largely in terms of economic efficiency. The argument increasingly revolved around the relative effectiveness of development strategies. The writers posed this question: what is the goal of development? And in their answers, we see the clear influence of mainstream of Western thinking on development. For many of these writers, beginning with Afghani, Islamic societies suffer from "backwardness" compared to the economies and societies of the West. Consequently, the target should be the "development" of Islamic societies along a trajectory that basically parallels the industrial and economic development paths of the Western world.

By entering into an argument about economic effectivity, most of these authors wind up making universal claims about the nature and potential of "Islamic economics." Not content with asserting the ethical superiority of an Islamic economic doctrine, they insist on making universal claims for the superiority of the "Islamic economy" in two ways.

First, it is claimed that the Islamic economy is more "realistic" than any other economic system, because it accords with universal human nature and tendencies. Although intended as a way of asserting the superiority of a distinctively Islamic program, this claim paradoxically threatens to dissolve the distinctiveness of "Islamic economics," since it is founded on a hypothetically verifiable claim, based on the universal category of "human nature." This differs little from the claim of the classical economists that they were simply describing and explaining how a certain system of economic organization best accorded with human nature.

This is generally followed by a second claim: an Islamic economy would be more efficient and less crisis-prone than a capitalist economy. However, these empirically testable claims for an "Islamic economy" place that economy directly on a par with the "economy" derived from the prescriptions of capitalism. In this comparison, Islamic economists have chosen to compete on the same ground. Significantly, however, this is not ground of Islam's making, but rather ground delineated by the capitalist economy.

The developmentalist paradigm increasingly invoked by the Islamic economists clearly derives from the particular dilemmas of the specific Muslim societies that need to be developed. Yet they evidently wish to retain the goal of building a truly Islamic society, a revived *umma*. The suspicion must be, however, that if the *umma* is to be revived by economic development prescriptions derived from the capitalist model — if, in other words, it is intended to compete with capitalism on capitalism's ground — it must itself be transformed into the kind of society that underpins the capitalist model of the economy.

Indeed, the paradox of this argument is demonstrated in the use which many of these writers make of the universal concept of "social welfare." It becomes clear from their writings that they are not simply talking of an Islamic society, but rather of a society of human individuals with broadly similar needs. In this connection, for instance, Baqir al-Sadr asserts that certain forms of activity may be "harmful to society" at various times in history, although they may be deemed less so at others.[7] Not only does this introduce the novel idea, for an Islamic writer, of the historical contingency of the good and the reprehensible. It also suggests that criteria of social welfare should be employed in the formulation of economic measures.

These are significant developments since they bring "society" into a prominent position as the arbiter of value. It is on the basis of *society's* needs, however interpreted, that the economy must be constructed. This is obviously a potentially open-ended and, for an Islamic program, dangerous development. If social needs are to form the basis for the construction of the economy — whether those needs are social justice or a certain level of material welfare — then its Islamic specificity must take second place.

In order to remedy this — to preserve something distinctively "Islamic" in this imagined economy and society — these writers have constructed the idea of the "Islamic individual," or the "Islamic personality" *(al-shakhsiyya al-islamiyya)*. This is presented as the basic unit of the Islamic economy, the *homo Islamicus* on which the perfectly balanced Islamic economy is to be grounded. Ultimately, the Islamic personality will guarantee the integrity of the Islamic economy. The individual Muslim's willingness to internalize the rules of the *shari'a* will ensure that social interest can never be at odds with Islamic obligation and that individual wants can never become the motive for unlimited acquisition. In other words, the "Islamic personality" is an ideal construct intended to form the self-regulating basis of the Islamic economy.[8]

There are problems in the ways in which this concept has been used. At times there is a suggestion that this is what Muslims are actually like, an essentialist demarcation of all Muslims from all other people. This leads to the assertion that there is something inalienable that will always insulate Muslims from the forces of capitalism and general Western influence. Yet there would be little purpose in delineating a specifically "Islamic economics" if all Muslims knew unfailingly how to act in accordance with the divine will and were thus armed individually against the many corruptions and seductions of capitalism.

At other times, the "Islamic personality" is used as a model of ethical probity towards which all individuals must aspire. The first task must be the construction of that personality, a process only at its inception. In some respects, this accords more with the worry of many of the writers about the effects of the modern world on Islamic identities and sensibilities. Precisely because Muslims are *not* immune to the power and seduction of capitalism, these writers feel it necessary to spell out the conditions for the nurturing of an Islamic personality.

Ironically, however, the target of this reform looks uncannily like the rational, calculating, hedonistic individual so beloved of economists and utilitarians. Indeed, the way *homo Islamicus* is supposed to take account of his or her Islamic obligations suggests an acceptance of the utilitarian criteria of interest and benefit calculation. The notion of an "Islamic calculus" is introduced. This means essentially that anyone calculating their pain or pleasure must take into account not simply the consequences in this world, but also those in the next, such as God's wrath or reward. This is asserted to be the solution to the "social problem" — a problem delineated, significantly enough, as the problem of trying to ensure that individuals make a "proper" calculation of the relative claims of their own interests when set against those of the society. Without such a calculation, the "social problem" will manifest itself as social disorder and instability.

The Islamic Bank

The other answer to the problem of reconciling economic effectivity with Islamic identity revolves around the idea of an "Islamic bank." Behind this idea there is obviously a more modest and perhaps potentially more realizable aim of creating space where an individual's principal economic transactions can take place within the rules of a recognizably Islamic framework. In other words, even if the community or the economic relations of society as a whole cannot be recreated in conformity with an imagined Islamic identity, at least individuals can begin to turn to an insulated zone of "Islamic" transactions. The individual thus resists succumbing, at least in one sphere, to un-Islamic, capitalist practices.

The Islamic bank was also seen as a way of forming *shari'a*-minded individuals for an imagined Islamic economic order. It would create and nurture the emerging *homo Islamicus*. However, the theoreticians recognized that the call to Islamic banking could not rest only on promises of ethical superiority. The Islamic bank was intended, after all, as a profitable and successful financial institution. Baqir al-Sadr, in his book *Iqtisaduna*, had already foreseen some of the dangers which might arise, since he speaks of the temptation to adapt the authoritative Islamic text *(nass)* to reality, rather than seeking to change reality on the basis of the text. He saw the danger that people might select and discard authoritative texts according to goals that were not specifically Islamic.[9]

The actual experience of Islamic banking, as it has emerged over the past few decades, would appear to have borne out some of his fears. Interpretations of Islamic obligation have been generally governed by criteria of financial success. Indeed, in the framework of a financial institution such as a bank, it could scarcely be otherwise. While Islamic banks claimed to be financial institutions aiming for development along ethical lines, they also claimed to realize greater profit for their investors. They may be operating within the conditions laid down and scrutinized by their *shari'a* supervisory boards, but they are also operating in competition with one another and are seeking to attract not simply the moral support of the believers, but also their capital. The latter is their raison d'être and will, in the final analysis, determine whether they survive.

Even some of their most well-disposed observers appear to be rightly skeptical of the degree to which the twenty or so years of Islamic banking have really contributed towards the wider aims of social responsibility and development that justified their establishment.[10] Indeed, the conclusion seems to be that their main achievement has been to strengthen themselves as financial institutions, but that in doing so they succumbed to a commercial logic that is hard to distinguish from the driving logic of capital accumulation. They have been recognized for their role in satisfying simultaneously the ethical and material aspirations of the individuals who are their depositors. But it is an open question whether this has strengthened the bonds of a distinctive Islamic order, or has merely reinforced the primacy of individualist, utilitarian calculations.

Conclusion: Towards Synthesis?

From this one can begin to see some of the ambiguity in the Islamic responses to capitalism. First, the terrain seems to have been already delineated and the terms themselves incorporated into the critique. Second, the logic of the argument is seriously affected — one might say compromised — by the terms of the debate and by the "logic" of capitalism itself. This becomes evident in any examination of the "solutions" to these problems.

However, this process and the responses which are associated with it also tell us something about the forms of Islam in the contemporary world, obliging us to think seriously about the degree to which Islamic thought, like any great system of ethics, may be influenced by the countervailing logic of other ethical systems with which its adherents must grapple if they are to preserve their own identity. As in this case, it is possible that the outcome will be more compromising and fragmented than those adherents may care to admit. A communicative logic, even a synthesis, may have established itself which can lead to accommodation. I have chosen to talk today about the Muslim encounter with the logic of capitalism, but there are other encounters — with the discourses of nationalism and democracy, for example — that are equally suggestive.

This process may also tell us something about the restiveness and frustration engendered by capitalism. Its capacity to inspire moral outrage cannot be denied. Furthermore, the idiom of its ethical indictment is readily at hand in Islam as in other pre-capitalist ethical and religious systems. The accountant looking out upon his disenchanted universe may find it incomprehensible that the ideals of religion have the power to capture and to move men's hearts, guiding their actions in this world. But large numbers of people are living in the dystopia that is the capitalist present, characterized by the subjective experiences of injustice, unequal distribution of wealth, social disintegration and environmental degradation.

In reaction to these experiences, a better future will be imagined. The fact that it may be unworkable will not necessarily dim its luster at moments of crisis. It may not have the power to deliver people from their fate, but it might provide them with a credo for concerted social action. That such imaginings persist in the Islamic world of the late twentieth century should remind us of the power of pre-capitalist values at this moment of liberal capitalism triumphant.

NOTES

1. See Noel W. Thompson, *The Market and its Critics* (London, 1988) and William Charlton, Tatiana Mallinson and Robert Oakeshott, *The Christian Response to Industrial Capitalism* (London, 1986).
2. Muhammad al-Ghazzali, *Al-Islam al-muftara alayhu bayna al-shuyu'iyyin wal-ra'smaliyyin* (Cairo, 1960), p. 14.
3. See for instance the Prophet's *hadith:* "Money is the trial *(fitna)* of my community."
4. In this group one could also include Khalid Muhammad Khalid, Muhammad Abu Zahra, Mustafa al-Zirqa and others linked to the publication *Al-Muslimun* (Cairo, 1952-54). A later figure who deals with similar issues and arrives at very similar conclusions is Hassan Hanafi in his serial publishing projects, *Al-Din wal-thawra* (Cairo, 1988-89) and *Min al-aqida ila al-thawra* (Cairo, 1988).
5. Sayyid Qutb, *Ma'alim fi al-tariq* (Cairo, 1988), especially pp. 14-23 and 165-77.
6. In the Arab world, one of the most interesting arenas for these debates was the journal *Al-Muslim al-mu'asir* (Beirut, 1974-86).
7. Muhammad Baqir al-Sadr, *Iqtisaduna* (Beirut, 1982), pp. 260-64.
8. Sadr, *Iqtisaduna*, p. 260; Syed Nawab Haidar Naqvi *Islam, Economics and Society* (London, 1994), pp. 13-19; Farhad Nomani and Ali Rahnema, *Islamic Economic Systems* (London, 1994), pp. 43-45, 84-91.
9. Sadr, *Iqtisaduna*, pp. 358-360
10. Aziz Alkazaz, "L'Islamisation du système bancaire et du système de financement au Pakistan," *Les Capitaux de l'Islam*, ed. Gilbert Beaugé (Paris, 1990), pp. 101-21; and Nomani and Rahnema, *Islamic Economic Systems*, pp. 162-86.

Islamic Economics and the "Clash of Civilizations"

by Timur Kuran

Everyone familiar with the social sciences knows that economics is concerned with phenomena like production, exchange, and consumption. Those who have studied economics know, in addition, that the discipline harbors diverse schools of thought — among them neoclassical economics and Marxian economics. The margins of the discipline are populated by lesser known schools, including several grounded in religion. And of the various schools of religious economics, the most influential has been one that characterizes itself as "Islamic economics." To prevent confusion, let me note immediately that only a small minority of all economists of the Muslim faith consider themselves "Islamic" economists. Yet this minority is politically significant.

Islamic economics emerged in the 1940s. Its declared purpose has been to identify and promote an economic order that conforms to Islamic scripture and traditions. For several decades, Islamic economics remained essentially an intellectual exercise. Since the 1970s, however, steps have been taken to give various economies an Islamic character. A few countries, including Pakistan, Saudi Arabia, and Malaysia, have instituted religious redistribution systems known as *zakat*. More than sixty countries now have Islamic banks that claim to offer an interest-free alternative to conventional banking. Several countries, notably Pakistan and Iran, have gone so far as to outlaw every form of interest. They are forcing all banks, including foreign subsidiaries, to adopt ostensibly Islamic financial methods.

The focus of this lecture will not be the specifics of Islamic economic thought or practice, although I will have to provide a few more details to substantiate my points. Rather, I am going to concentrate on why Islamic economics emerged, why it continues to enjoy some appeal, and why its significance goes much beyond economics.[1]

It has been argued that Islamic economics is incoherent, incomplete, and impractical.[2] On this basis, questions have been raised about why anyone would believe that Islamic economics is capable of raising productivity, stimulating growth, or reducing inequality. A major part of my response is that the main purpose of Islamic economics is not to improve economic performance. Notwithstanding the stated aspiration to provide a superior alternative to other economic doctrines, its real purpose is to help prevent Muslims from assimilating into the emerging global culture whose core has a Western pedigree. The *economics* of Islamic economics is secondary to its *Islamic* character; its essential function is to foster a sense of Muslim cultural separateness and to protect Muslim cultures.

Moreover, in pursuing cultural separatism and protectionism, Islamic economics depends only minimally on controlling Muslim behaviors in the marketplace. I shall argue that its chief instrument for fighting assimilation is the guilt that it fosters by characterizing certain universal economic practices as un-Islamic. Guilt-ridden Muslims, seeking atonement for economic behaviors they perceive as possibly sinful, contribute to religious causes, support religious movements, and undertake acts of religious piety. In the process, they inflate the observed religiosity of the Muslim world. And they magnify the apparent constituency for extending Islam's temporal domain and authority.

The Substance of Islamic Economics

Before I develop the argument that Islamic economics serves as an instrument of cultural politics, let me say a bit more about its substance and its practical applications.

One of the distinguishing features of Islamic economics is that it treats communalist values as critical to an economic system's operation. The prevailing economic systems of our time are all failures, it maintains, because they neglect the moral dimensions of human existence. For example, capitalist systems seek social efficiency mainly through actions motivated by self-interest, and for this reason they are beset by high unemployment, pollution, and rampant poverty; and regulations to correct the shortcomings of capitalism are often ineffective because those who implement them are guided by the wrong values. Islamic economics insists that in a society whose members are infused with Islamic values, the flaws of capitalism will be absent. Consider the universal problem of pollution. Pollution will be minimal in an Islamic society, it is maintained, because people steeped in communalist values will voluntarily refrain from harming the environment. Coercive measures or market incentives will be needed only to bring in line the morally deficient, whose numbers in any case will be small.

A related complaint about the prevailing economic systems is that they feature rampant opportunism, dishonesty, and mistrust. All over the world, so goes the argument, people frequently get cheated in the marketplace. Aware of the risks of participating in exchange, they remain always on guard against unscrupulous dealers, clients, and partners. The situation imposes costs on them, and it encourages them to become cheaters themselves. And the resulting vicious circle keeps the economy inhospitable to business, with adverse effects on employment and investment. The root cause of the vicious circle, Islamic economics argues, is the selfishness inspired by Western individualism. Dishonesty would be less frequent if people had more concern for others and for society as a whole. Yet there is not much evidence that the recent emphasis on fostering a communalist, non-individualistic morality and on combating selfishness has improved the business climate in the Islamic world. Significantly, contributions to Islamic economics continue to claim that corruption and cheating remain terrible problems.

In addition to moral reforms, Islamic economics proposes certain institutional reforms based on the traditional sources of Islam. Most importantly, the entire financial system is to be overhauled through the replacement of conventional banks by Islamic banks. The difference between the two types of banks is that properly Islamic banks avoid interest. If you borrow funds from an Islamic bank to finance a business venture, the bank cannot, as a conventional bank might, charge you interest on the loan. It can accept a share of your potential profits, along with a share of your losses in the event your project is unsuccessful. Islamic banking, say its proponents, makes saving more attractive by giving savers opportunities to share in the profits of investors; it also channels funds to entrepreneurs without a credit history. As such, it helps solve two major problems: low growth and maldistribution.

So much for the alleged virtues of Islamic banking. What of the practice? The Islamic banks are roughly as profitable as their conventional counterparts, and they are making positive contributions to various economies. But in no way have they revolutionized financial practices. Even the leading advocates of Islamic banking now admit that the Islamic banks give and take interest as a matter of course, often through clever ruses designed to make interest look like profit. They are not channeling funds primarily to new entrepreneurs; in fact, many are ultra-conservative in their lending practices. Here and there the Islamic banks have introduced a few innovations, but these hardly form a radically new financial system.

The last major element of the program to overhaul the economic system according to Islamic prescriptions is the revival and strengthening of *zakat*. *Zakat* is a redistribution system that was present in Arabia fourteen centuries ago, in the early years of Islam. A huge contemporary literature claims that *zakat* will provide a more effective safety net than the existing secular redistribution programs. Yet the official *zakat* systems instituted in various places have not lived up to expectations. In Pakistan, the official *zakat* system does not even meet the subsistence needs of the small minority of the poor that it assists. In Malaysia, *zakat* produces perverse redistribution, in that it collects funds primarily from poor peasants and spends them on often wealthier government workers living in the cities (although the perversity is now being dampened through greater urban collections). In both Pakistan and Malaysia, there have been reports, including official reports, of serious irregularities in both collection and disbursement. It is true, of course, that in both Muslim and non-Muslim societies irregularities beset secular redistribution systems, too. But Islamic economics promises to do much better.

The key points of this cursory overview are two. First, Islamic economics does not amount to a radically new school of thought. And second, its applications, though generally not harmful and sometimes beneficial from a narrowly economic standpoint, have not brought major changes to economic life. How, then, do we make sense of its emergence and continuing popularity? The answer that I will now develop is, once again, that Islamic economics is driven by cultural rather than economic concerns.

The Cultural Functions of Islamic Economics

A telling indication that Islamic economics is driven mainly by cultural concerns is that its founders were Muslim Indians striving to justify why they should have cultural autonomy and even their own state. Sayyid Abul A'la Maududi, the social activist who coined the term "Islamic economics" around the time of India's partition, argued in his writings that intensified contacts with Westerners were destroying Muslim cultures.

Western secularism was about to lock Islam in the mosque, he maintained; it was making the Indian part of the Muslim-Indian identity eclipse the Muslim part. Even worse, secularism was turning Muslims into pseudo-Muslims with mindsets and lifestyles indistinguishable from those of Westerners. Maududi thought these dangers to Islam could be fought by resisting the universalization of human morality. Muslims would not be so eager to Indianize and Westernize if they were made to see that Islamic and non-Islamic values, including economic values, are incompatible.[3]

In the decades following Maududi's initial writings, Pakistanis have made by far the largest share of contributions to Islamic economics. In a bibliography that leads up to 1975,[4] about 70 percent of the contributions to Islamic economics are by Pakistanis. The share of non-Pakistani contributions has grown since then, but that of South Asians continues to dominate.[5] Had economic concerns been the principal force behind the rise of Islamic economics, writers from other countries might have had better representation among the early contributors. But Pakistan is the world's only state founded with the express purpose of giving Muslims a place where they can govern themselves according to Islamic prescriptions and priorities. Concerns about culture were actually more significant, which explains Pakistan's critical role.

After the emergence of Islamic economics in the Indian subcontinent, new circumstances gave it additional pushes. Most importantly, the oil price jumps of the 1970s created a need to recirculate massive sums of Arab petrodollars, and the first Islamic banks were founded at this time to help the process in a politically acceptable manner. It is at this time that the institutional infrastructure of Islamic economics got a huge boost from the oil-rich Arab regimes. Yet the point remains that even today, people from the Indian subcontinent play disproportionate roles in both the formulation and the practice of Islamic economics.

Also revealing is the methodology of Islamic economics. The typical text combs traditional sources for prescriptions that will differentiate Islamic economics from other economic doctrines and systems. The blanket prohibition of interest ostensibly found in the Qur'an is just such a prescription because interest plays an important role in every contemporary economic doctrine and every actual economy. By favoring a categorical ban on interest, Islamic economics can claim that the deposit-taking and lending operations of "Islamic banks" differ fundamentally from those of conventional banks.

Yet another sign that the driving force of Islamic economics is cultural identity lies in the attention that many texts give to issues of negligible importance to modern readers. Barter rules, the rights of slaves, the permissibility of selling fruit trees in bloom, and rules concerning other such transactions foreign to twentieth-century readers make prominent appearances in contributions to Islamic economics, simply because they receive broad coverage in classical Islamic sources. At the same time, Islamic economics has contributed little to certain economic issues of great relevance to modern living. As far as I know, there is no distinctly Islamic position on how firms should respond to new technologies that put people out of work. The substantive contributions of Islamic economics have been limited even in Pakistan and Iran, the countries that have gone farthest in putting Islamic economics into practice.

It is important to recognize that early Islamic civilization was the fount of much economic creativity. For example, the Muslim jurists of the seventh through tenth centuries helped codify investment practices that had an influence on the evolution of contract law in Western Europe.[6] And they set various rules aimed at mitigating mistrust between buyer and seller. The ban on selling fruit trees in bloom was just such a rule: in the absence of insurance markets we now take for granted, it minimized differences between the expectations of buyer and seller.

But it is one thing to make sense of old values and institutions, and to recognize their important contributions to global economic evolution, quite another to see them as solutions to today's problems. Mistrust between buyers and sellers is certainly a factor that inhibits trade, investment, and growth all over the world, and certainly in the Middle East. But the solution to this economic problem must be informed by contemporary conditions; rules developed in medieval times are likely to fall short. If medieval texts *are* being combed for answers, it is because the primary goal is to cultivate a separate identity, rather than to produce viable answers.

There is an additional sign that the purpose of Islamic economics is essentially cultural. If its prescriptions were driven primarily by economic concerns, it would be forming bridges to non-Islamic intellectual traditions that are searching for alternatives to prevailing economic systems. In particular, it would be showing an interest in modern research programs that explore the origins, consequences, and dynamics of economic values.[7] But Islamic economics has hardly sought to benefit from non-Islamic research on morality. The reason, I would suggest, is that recognizing the universality of its basic moral concerns would defeat the objective of cultivating a separate Muslim identity.

Clashing Civilizations: Islam vs. the West

There is nothing, of course, inherently Islamic about trying to reduce mistrust between traders or about trying to foster honesty. Every society takes measures to these ends. Standardization systems and warranty systems are among the institutions used everywhere to foster trust between buyers and sellers. Nor, to go further, is there anything intrinsically Islamic or intrinsically anti-Western about proposing restrictions on interest. Certain arguments against interest-based commercial lending could easily be incorporated into secular economic discourse.[8] Indeed, stripped of its Islamic vocabulary and imagery, a proposal to ban interest-based finance could be evaluated by the same standards through which secular economists assess the merits of subjecting banks to reserve requirements. If the drive against interest happens to carry strong anti-Western overtones, this is only because of incessant efforts to associate the practice with un-Islamic, Western materialism.

The payment of interest is not the only economic practice that many Islamic economists find un-Islamic. Others include insurance, arbitrage, speculation, and indexation.[9] The typical text in Islamic economics is replete with injunctions to avoid this or that behavior, often on the grounds that, in the author's reading, the Qur'an or some other source of religious authority rules against it. From Maududi onwards, the moral discourse of Islamic economics has cultivated the view that the behavioral standards of Islam are fundamentally at odds with non-Islamic, especially Western, ones. This moral discourse impinges on a controversy launched by Samuel Huntington's thesis that the dominant source of global conflict is now culture rather than ideology or economics. The centerpiece of international politics, says Huntington, is now "the interaction between the West and non-Western civilizations and among non-Western civilizations."[10] In terms of Huntingon's thesis, the moral discourse of Islamic economics may be seen as an effort to segregate Islamic civilization from non-Islamic ones.

Huntington's thesis has come under fire for underestimating the homogenizing effect of economic development and for overlooking most people's receptivity to cross-cultural influences. It is true that social transformations like urbanization, industrialization, and modern education are attenuating the differences between non-Western and Western lifestyles. But this does not negate the fact that such transformations have fueled movements of cultural resistance. Precisely because these transformations have been so disruptive to traditional lifestyles, campaigns to protect local mores, beliefs, values, and institutions are commonplace everywhere. Huntington's thesis has also been criticized on the grounds that civilizations are difficult to define. The boundaries among civilizations are indeed somewhat arbitrary, and every major civilization harbors much diversity. Yet these facts do not keep cultural protectionists of various stripes from acting as if the civilizations they want to preserve are well-defined entities. There are vast differences between the lifestyles of secularized Muslims in Istanbul and devout Muslims in Kelantan, between life in a Bengali village and life in the royal palaces of Arabia. Yet Islamist activists commonly ignore such differences.

Whatever the shortcomings of Huntington's thesis, the Islamists, whose ranks include the promoters of Islamic economics, share Huntington's view that international politics revolves around the interaction of civilizations. From Maududi onwards, they have taken every opportunity to promote stronger social and economic bonds among Muslim communities, hoping that these will pave the way for an Islamic common market and, ultimately, a pan-Islamic state.[11] A complementary objective of Islamism has been to weaken commercial and industrial ties between the Muslim world and the West, in order to protect Muslims from un-Islamic cultural influences.

Here lies a major inconsistency: the objective of a self-segregating pan-Islamic union is at odds with the communalist morality advocated by Islamic economics. This morality includes, in addition to restrictions that would hinder complex economic linkages, a major emphasis on generosity and voluntary communal cooperation as vehicles for solving social problems. In essence, therefore, it is the communalist morality of medieval Islamic civilization. This morality encouraged individuals to interact primarily with members of their own local communities, defined geographically, religiously, and ethnically; and it made them rely on communal sanctions to foster trust and settle disputes.[12]

By contrast, from the same starting point, medieval Western Europe gradually developed an individualist morality, which limited the economic significance of subgroup identities and facilitated interactions across subgroup boundaries.[13] This individualist morality fostered, as a substitute for generosity and subgroup pressures, the evolution of modern economic institutions like corporate contract law and standardization boards. Moreover, after the Middle Ages, the difference in moral systems contributed to Europe's growing economic dominance over the Islamic world. Long-distance trade between the two worlds came to be conducted increasingly by Europeans and their agents, because they, unlike Muslim traders, enjoyed the appropriate institutional support.

From these observations, it follows that in seeking to revive the communalist economic morality responsible for the Muslim world's ongoing underdevelopment, Islamic economics is actually thwarting its stated goal of improving living standards. Nor is it preparing Muslims for an Islamic common market: the values that Islamic economics seeks to reinstitute would hinder, not facilitate, linkages among diverse Muslim communities. If establishing an Islamic common market is the goal, the most effective way of pursuing that goal would be to strengthen legal and economic institutions that allow distant traders — Malay exporters and Tunisian importers — to do business with confidence.

The civilizational clash that Islamic economics is encouraging is often misconstrued as a collision of old and new. The values of Islamic economics are indeed firmly rooted in moral traditions. But the objective of ending the Muslim world's political and economic fragmentation represents an effort to break rather than strengthen tradition. Trade among Muslim countries is limited, except in oil. So an increase in non-oil trade within the Islamic world would represent a major departure from the present. True, an Islamic precedent exists even for this attempt at reform. As a matter of principle, the first Islamic state in seventh-century Arabia discouraged the segmentation of Muslims on the basis of ethnicity, language, or geography. In practice, however, neither the first Islamic state nor its successors managed to obliterate the social significance of tribal, ethnic, linguistic, sectarian, geographic, and other divisions — a point made forcefully in Ibn Khaldun's fourteenth-century *Muqaddimah*.[14] In trying to strengthen the Islamic identity of Muslim communities as a means of breaking their nonreligious solidarity patterns, today's Islamists are attempting, then, to perform a task at which even the earliest Muslims failed. That the fundamentalist strategy is self-defeating does not negate its revolutionary element.

Thus far, I have argued that for cultural reasons, Islamic economics is seeking to revive an old economic morality. I have argued, secondly, that Islamic economics supports a reformist geopolitical agenda aimed at ending the current fragmentation of the Islamic world. Finally, I have suggested that these two goals — cultural revival and political union — are contradictory. Let me now explore whether and how these efforts are resonating with individual Muslims.

Clashing Selves: Homo Islamicus vs. Homo Economicus

The objective of overcoming the Muslim world's fragmentation reflects, in part, an understanding that the traditional economic structures of Muslim communities are no longer sustainable. Most individual Muslims share this understanding. They realize that still-surviving traditional economic structures will inevitably succumb to the forces unleashed by the Industrial Revolution. They recognize, too, that to become prosperous themselves they must engage in practices, like dealing in interest, that Islamic economics portrays as immoral. At the same time, they take pride in the achievements of their cultures, and they want religion to play some role in their lives. These two goals — advancing economically and following what is considered a properly Islamic lifestyle — are not always in harmony. The consequent tensions are all the more serious because Islamic economics makes Muslims' inevitable economic adaptations seem in conflict with maintaining an Islamic identity. One of the effects of Islamic economics is thus to promote clashes within individual Muslims — clashes that pit the *homo economicus* within them against the *homo Islamicus.*

Wherever there is discomfort, efforts will be made to alleviate it. Experiments by social psychologists show that individuals led to feel they have harmed others subsequently strive to rehabilitate themselves. In the simplest of these experiments, subjects who were made to believe that they broke a camera while walking through a store became dramatically more willing, relative to the control group, to help someone in need.[15] From our standpoint here, it is significant that the individuals who thought they had caused damage sought to expiate their guilt by becoming more helpful toward others in general, rather than specifically toward owners of the purportedly broken camera.

Such psychological experiments shed light on the observed responses to Islamic economics. Individuals who feel compelled to engage in economic practices portrayed as immoral can seek to exonerate themselves through various acts of altruism. Yet the most effective way to make amends for perceived transgressions against Islam is to undertake acts that carry Islamic significance. The possibilities include joining public prayers, making donations to mosques, participating in Islamic political rallies, and wearing clothes that symbolize Islamic piety. The upshot is that medieval economic injunctions, when revived centuries later in settings where they pose a nuisance, will have the effect not of changing economic behavior but of promoting various forms of religious participation.

As I mentioned earlier, Islamic economists never tire of pointing out that contemporary Muslim communities are rife with greed, corruption, dishonesty, deceit, and exploitation.[16] My own view is that these problems will not disappear simply through praises of Islamic virtue. In the absence of institutional reforms that make socially undesirable behaviors more costly — improvements in the legal system, industrial standardization, removal of anti-competitive regulations — the problems will persist. Moreover, the main effect of turning a spotlight on them will be to make individual Muslims ever more conscious of their moral failings. Guilt-ridden, many will seek to compensate for their moral deficiencies through greater outward piety.

This reasoning speaks to a puzzling aspect of the record of Islamic banking. The puzzle is that the banks have spread and grown even though their operations are based, for all practical purposes, on interest. If my reasoning is correct, one of the factors in this popularity must be that the banks serve as an instrument of guilt reduction for depositors and borrowers who believe that, even if they are not actually interest-free, they are at least morally superior to conventional banking. The Islamic banks foster an image of moral superiority by making a point of contributing to Islamic causes and also through signs of Islamic devotion at their branch offices: prayer areas, Qur'anic verses on the walls, veiled female and bearded male tellers, religious literature for the taking.

If one way that Islamic economics provokes guilt is through injunctions that are costly to follow, another is through its own inconsistencies. Islamic economists disagree among themselves on many substantive matters, and their programs contain contradictions.[17] The basic reason for the tensions is that the fundamental sources of Islam themselves harbor many inconsistencies. To give just one basic example, some recollections of the Prophet Muhammad's sayings make it seem that Islam rejects all interference with market freedoms. Yet classical Islamic texts contain other accounts that contradict the sacredness of market outcomes, and Islamic history offers numerous precedents for tight economic regulation. The essential implication here is that a Muslim determined to abide by all Islamic injunctions will find it impossible to pursue a life that is properly Islamic beyond all doubt. Consequently, he will fail to escape guilt.

The Significance of Islamic Economic Morality

It is time to tie up the threads of this argument. Secular economists, both Muslim and non-Muslim, have greeted Islamic economics with contempt and ridicule. Yet, like religion in general, Islamic economics is a force capable of moving huge numbers of intelligent and educated people. If my argument is correct, however, what gets moved will not necessarily be economic behavior. People can substitute non-economic forms of religious participation for the economic ones demanded of them.

Many centuries ago, the communalist economic morality being promoted by Islamic economists accommodated growth within societies that, by modern standards, were economically primitive. Under present global conditions, that same morality would limit individual and collective enrichment, yet also promote a stronger Islamic identity. There is no evidence that more than a small fraction of all Muslims are prepared to accept such a tradeoff. Just as contemporary Italians are happy to use Arabic numerals rather than the more cumbersome Roman ones, most Muslims are quite prepared to use financial and commercial mechanisms developed in the West.

Yet many consider their identity under threat, not the least because Islamists treat various moral and institutional adaptations as evidence of cultural capitulation. Consequently, even some who are able to justify their own economic adaptations are wondering whether they might be contributing to the erosion of their society's Islamic identity. Insofar as they want that identity preserved, they experience psychological tensions. Seeking peace, they try to compensate for their questionable behaviors through acts that symbolize Islamic defiance and separatism. They thus end up serving the anti-assimilationist goal of Islamism. Paradoxically, this occurs because under modern conditions it is impossible to live up to the moral ideals of Islamism in general and Islamic economics in particular.

The significance of the steps taken to give economies an Islamic character lies only partially, then, in their economic content. Much of their importance lies in their symbolism, in their implications for the present and future distribution of political power, and in their cultural meaning. Remember that Maududi's aim was not to galvanize a radical shift in economic thought or unleash a revolution in economic practices. His aim was to reaffirm Islam's relevance to modern life and to preserve Islamic identity. From the standpoint of Maududi's objectives, the ongoing economic activities represent an accomplishment. They invoke Islamic authority in a domain that modern civilization has secularized. And by making people feel a need to assert their religious identity, they help erect and strengthen cultural boundaries.

NOTES

1. Some of the ideas developed in this lecture appeared in a brief address I gave to the American Economic Association in January 1996: "The Discontents of Islamic Economic Morality," *American Economic Review*, vol. 86, no. 2 (May 1996): 438-42.
2. See, for example, Sohrab Behdad, "Property Rights in Contemporary Islamic Economic Thought: A Critical Perspective," *Review of Social Economy*, vol. 47, no. 2 (Summer 1989): 185-211; and Timur Kuran, "The Economic Impact of Islamic Fundamentalism," in *Fundamentalisms and the State: Remaking Polities, Economies, and Militance*, eds. Martin E. Marty and R. Scott Appleby (Chicago, 1993), pp. 302-41.
3. Seyyed Vali Reza Nasr, *Mawdudi and the Making of Islamic Revivalism* (Oxford, 1996).
4. Muhammad Nejatullah Siddiqi, *Muslim Economic Thinking: A Survey of Contemporary Literature* (Leicester, 1981).
5. Thomas Philipp, "The Idea of Islamic Economics," *Die Welt des Islams*, vol. 30 (1990): 117-39, at 117.
6. Abraham L. Udovitch, *Partnership and Profit in Medieval Islam* (Princeton, 1970).
7. These include Robert H. Frank, *Passions within Reason: The Strategic Role of the Emotions* (New York, 1988); and James Q. Wilson, *The Moral Sense* (New York, 1993).
8. For some prominent arguments in favor of banning interest, see M. Umer Chapra, *Towards a Just Monetary System* (Leicester, 1985).

9. Mohammed Abdul Mannan, *Islamic Economics: Theory and Practice* (Lahore, 1970); and M. Umer Chapra, *Islam and the Economic Challenge* (Leicester, 1992).
10. Samuel P. Huntington, "The Clash of Civilizations?" *Foreign Affairs*, vol. 72, no. 3 (Summer 1993): 22-49, quote at 23.
11. For arguments in favor of a common market, see Masudul Alam Choudhury, *Islamic Economic Co-operation* (New York, 1989).
12. Avner Greif, "Cultural Beliefs and the Organization of Society: A Historical and Theoretical Reflection on Collectivist and Individualist Societies," *Journal of Political Economy*, vol. 102, no. 5 (October 1994): 912-50.
13. Albert O. Hirschman, *The Passions and the Interests: Political Arguments for Capitalism before Its Triumph* (Princeton, 1977); Greif, "Cultural Beliefs"; Michael Oakeshott, *Morality and Politics in Modern Europe: The Harvard Lectures*, ed. Shirley Robin Letwin (New Haven, 1993 [lectures delivered in 1958]); and Nathan Rosenberg and L. E. Birdzell, Jr., *How the West Grew Rich: The Economic Transformation of the Industrial World* (New York, 1986), esp. chap. 4.
14. Ibn Khaldun, *The Muqaddimah: An Introduction to History*, transl. Franz Rosenthal (3 vols.; Princeton, 1957).
15. Dennis Regan, Margo Williams, and Sondra Sparling, "Voluntary Expiation of Guilt: A Field Experiement," *Journal of Personality and Social Psychology*, vol. 24, no. 1 (October 1972): 42-45.
16. See, for example, Chapra, *Islam and the Economic Challenge*.
17. Timur Kuran, "On the Notion of Economic Justice in Contemporary Islamic Thought," *International Journal of Middle East Studies*, vol. 21, no. 2 (May 1989): 171-91.

The Charismatic Islamists

by Judith Miller

As an American journalist who has long worked in the Arab Middle East, I have been fortunate in having had firsthand exposure to many leaders of militant Islamic movements. It is my impressions of these men — and the leaders are invariably male — that I shall discuss today, to explore how their social background, education, personality and political culture have affected their movements. In so doing, I will make generalizations that I try to avoid in my book, wary as I am of the often misleading stereotypes about Islamism fed partly by the media, but also by many scholars.[1] Nevertheless, I have concluded that despite their ostensible differences, three of the men I have studied — Hasan al-Turabi of Sudan, Sayyid Muhammad Husayn Fadlallah of Lebanon, and Abdolkarim Sorush of Iran — share some strikingly similar traits.

First of all, they are all charismatic. That is, they are people who exude a moral authority that is politically persuasive to a great many people in their respective societies, particularly to the "downtrodden," as they are called: those who are poor and often semi-educated, and who harbor deep resentment over the broken promises of their autocratic and enduring regimes. This is particularly true of Hasan al-Turabi, the de facto ruler of the Islamic Republic of Sudan, whose militant National Islamic Front (NIF), a branch of the Muslim Brotherhood, seized power in a military coup in 1989.

I first met Turabi in the early 1980s. He was then, and remains an intellectually impressive man, a doctor of law — not a shaykh — educated in London and Paris, fluent in at least three languages (and possibly four, if one ignores his modest claim of speaking only "adequate" German). Sixty-four years old, he looks much younger. He is tall, thin, and suave. He seems equally at ease in his half-foot-high white turban and his Saville Row, double-breasted suit, a claim that most Middle Eastern leaders can hardly make given the region's rich diet. He is particularly adept in speaking (in any language) to Western journalists, for whom he usually makes time.

In the early 1980s, Turabi was the Western journalists' favorite "enlightened" Islamist. He said everything we wanted to hear. He talked about the need to emancipate women, greater political and cultural pluralism in Arab societies, his respect for Western democracies and for the West in general. I was not alone in being impressed with what the "Turabi in opposition" said. One of his acolytes, Abdelwahab El-Affendi, a Sudanese political scientist, turned his Ph.D. dissertation, a biography of Turabi, into a book — the only such published work in English — which praised the Sudanese Muslim Brotherhood leader as the chief promoter of a new, modern, and decidedly pragmatic Islamism capable of resolving many of the problems that have long plagued Sudan.

Turabi in Power

But as we soon saw, Turabi's discourse changed dramatically after his NIF seized power. In my later interviews with him, Sudan's self-styled militant Islamic "democrat" had a radically new line: Western-style democracy, with its political parties and open elections, he said, would be no more than a sham given Sudan's corrupt, tribal-based party structure. Democracy would deteriorate into an exercise in clan politics, and so was undesirable. Yes, women had to be emancipated, but within an "Islamic" framework. Religious minorities had to be tolerated, but within the context of the shari'a, Islam's holy law. Turabi's philosophy shifted so radically and rapidly that El-Affendi, then working as a cultural attaché in the Sudanese embassy in London, published a second book only a few months after his first, entitled Who Needs an Islamic State? The book, I believe, reflects the author's disenchantment with both his former hero and the "Islamic" regime over which Turabi presides. El-Affendi himself has now left Sudanese government service, preferring the intellectually independent if more impoverished life of a part-time professor and journalist in England.

Turabi, like so many other militant leaders, is also a man of enormous ego. After Sudan's former martial arts champion nearly killed him with karate chops to the head in a Canadian airport in 1992, Turabi's sense of destiny was strengthened. His very survival had made him a "symbol of Islam," he told me. He had been spared for a God-sanctioned, if not God-given mission: to take power and keep it until his particular Islamic vision is fulfilled. Sudan is now paying a high price for his politico-religious egomania.

A third aspect of his personality — again shared by several other militant leaders — is his extraordinary shrewdness and political pragmatism. It was Turabi who sensed early on, for example, that a close affiliation between the Sudanese branch of the Muslim Brotherhood and the "mother" branch in Cairo would be problematic in a country that had been repeatedly invaded by Egypt. Historically, Sudanese had not only been enslaved and oppressed by their lighter-skinned Egyptian neighbors, they had been intellectually patronized. So early on, Turabi distanced his movement from Cairo. He changed the group's name and declared doctrinal and political independence from the Muslim Brotherhood of Egypt. Each Islamic movement, Turabi said, had to express itself in its own cultural and political idiom. In so doing, Turabi split the Sudanese Brotherhood into two warring factions. But the divorce from Egypt proved a brilliant stroke, for Turabi's faction eventually triumphed, both within the movement and, later, within Sudan.

A second innovation was his rejection of the traditional Muslim Brotherhood preference for education, social welfare, and moral example as the primary means of creating an Islamic society, which in turn, Muslim Brotherhood stalwarts argued, would result in the inevitable creation of "Islamic" governments. He rejected the view that Muslims had to develop their own alternative society within the "infidel" society. His motto, instead, was "strike a blow for Islam, whenever, wherever you can." So his followers never missed an opportunity to fill a government post, work in a powerful bank, or most important of all, join the security services and the military. While other Islamist parties shunned the "pseudo-Islamic" military regime of General Ja'far al-Numayri, Turabi's Brotherhood joined it. As a result, although his NIF never secured more than 20 percent of the vote in national elections, his recruits were eventually well enough positioned to seize power through a military coup.

For Turabi, consistency is no virtue. Sudan's Islamic leader has been consistent in only one respect: he has demonstrated that he is prepared to say or do anything to hold onto power. If that means becoming an adept liar — denying, for example, that there are "ghost houses" in Khartoum in which political opponents disappear and are tortured, or that Arabs have enslaved black Sudanese from the south — so be it. If it means denying that his country has become a haven for terrorists — a place to secure "a shower and a shave," as one American diplomat put it — so be it. And like so many other Islamist leaders, while he speaks about a worldwide Islamic *umma*, his primary interest is not Arab and Islamic unity, or defeating Israel and challenging the West, but perpetuating his own vision of "Islamic" rule in Sudan.[2]

Ayatollah Fadlallah

Many of these characteristics are shared by Sayyid Fadlallah, four years younger at age sixty than Sudan's Islamic Svengali, and also a charismatic man. Although he is not as physically imposing as Turabi — in fact, with his white whiskers, sparkling eyes and roly-poly frame, he resembles an Islamic Santa Claus — he is a far more gifted orator than Turabi. Also unlike Turabi, Fadlallah is a first-rate scholar and prolific writer of Arabic poetry and prose. Although he speaks no language but Arabic, he is as astute as Turabi in understanding what Westerners want to hear and what his movement, Hizbullah, must do to survive and grow stronger.

Like Turabi, he has an enormous ego. When I asked him whether Ayatollah Khamenei, Iran's supreme guide, should be the *marja' al-taqlid* of all the world's Shiites, Fadlallah declared that while Iranians might well follow Khamenei's political and spiritual lead, Shiites outside of Iran — say, those in Lebanon, the only Arab country other than Bahrain where Shiites outnumber Sunni Muslims — were not bound to emulate Khamenei. Fadlallah, or Ayatollah Fadlallah as he told me he prefers to be addressed, chafes at comparisons between himself, the author of more than one hundred books, and the Iranian leader, who was made an instant ayatollah only days after Khomeini died, a scholar who never even presented his *risala*, the book-length thesis required of all real ayatollahs. In our most recent interview, Fadlallah repeatedly rejected Khamenei's claims to spiritual and political leadership over non-Iranian Shiites, and of Hizbullah in particular.[3] Fadlallah resents Iran's diktats to believers in Lebanon; he sees himself as the natural intellectual and ideological leader of Lebanon's Shiite flock, who now constitute some 40 percent of Lebanon's inhabitants and the country's largest single religious group.

Despite the organization's financial dependence on Iran, Fadlallah has fought hard to preserve some of Hizbullah's political independence from Iran. It was he who persuaded the Iranian government, he told me, to bless Hizbullah's entry into Lebanon's parliamentary election fray in 1992. There were other ways — better ways, he implied — to spread Islam than the revolution launched by Khomeini's followers in 1979. In

Lebanon, Hizbullah could use the election system to strike a blow for Islam. As a result of those elections, Hizbullah has become more than a social welfare support network or Katyusha-waiving zealots. They are among the most important blocs in parliament, part of Lebanon's political establishment — insurance, Fadlallah implied, against the day when Iran or Syria might find Hizbullah's anti-Israeli fighting militias expendable.

Also like Turabi, Fadlallah has evolved and demonstrated impressive political pragmatism. Once committed to the immediate eradication of the Zionist entity and creation of an Islamic state in Lebanon, Fadlallah in recent interviews has distanced himself from both objectives. Vowing to impose Islam on Lebanon's many religious and ethnic sects merely complicated efforts to form coalitions in parliament in order to advance Hizbullah's political agenda. There was no reason to create fear about the inevitable, Fadlallah suggested. Demography is on Hizbullah's side: Christians were still leaving Lebanon in droves; the Shiites were still growing; and Amal, once Hizbullah's formidable competitor, had fewer and fewer roots. Eventually, Lebanon would become an Islamic state, led, inevitably in Fadlallah's view, by the organization he guides, but over which he, like Turabi, denies any official leadership.

With respect to Israel, a fall-back position was also essential if Hizbullah were to remain politically relevant. As secular Arab leaders translated the Oslo peace process into treaties with Israel after 1993, Fadlallah reformulated Hizbullah's anti-Zionist goal: preventing Lebanese-Israeli normalization, a far more realistic aim.

Finally, Fadlallah, like Turabi, is a fatalist who equates his own survival with God's grand design and evidence of the inevitability of his ideology's triumph. A plot by rogue ex-CIA operatives to blow him up outside his mosque in the mid-1980s left more than eighty believers dead and scores more wounded. But Fadlallah, who was delayed that day by a woman parishioner, was nowhere near the site during the blast.

Sorush's Dissent

The third militant Islamist leader who has survived enormous challenges and evolved into a dramatically different political figure than he was a decade ago is Abdolkarim Sorush, fifty years old, an unofficial leader of Iran's Islamic opposition, its home-grown Martin Luther who is promoting what some scholars have called an Islamic reformation in the Islamic Republic of Iran.

I was skeptical of Sorush before meeting him in the fall of 1995 in Teheran. While his recent essays argued passionately and persuasively for the need for reform in Iran, Sorush had not always been the Islamic liberal he claims to be today. Early on in the revolution, Iranians told me, he was a senior member of the cultural revolutionary committee at the university in Teheran, a zealot who helped purge roughly two-thirds of the faculty and supervised the burning of books deemed offensive to Islam. Yet seventeen years of experience with the Islamic regime had convinced him, he suggested, that Islam would die — at least in its Iranian form — if it did not return to people's hearts by retreating from politics to the mosque, from the political capital of Teheran to the Islamic seat of learning in Qom. Without reform, he told me, the Islamic project in Iran was doomed. So to save Islam, people like him had to distance themselves from the regime, if not from the revolution that inspired it, by criticizing its many errors.

Sorush, now a militant Islamist in opposition, as Turabi once was and Fadlallah remains, must couch his argument subtly and carefully. He rarely attacks the regime overtly. To do so increases risk in Iran's autocratic state, which, while it tolerates far more criticism than most of its secular Arab counterparts, insists that criticism occur within an Islamic framework. So instead of attacking the regime frontally, Sorush emphasizes philosophical themes, such as Islam's relativism, a concept that the regime rejects. There can be no absolute truth, he argues, because Islam, God's creation, ultimately came to be interpreted by men. As such, Islam, by definition, must be relative, and hence pluralistic, democratic in spirit, open to change, and subject to perpetual *ijtihad*, or interpretation by knowledgeable persons.

Like Turabi and Fadlallah, he is fatalistic about the repeated attacks on him, assaults during lectures and seminars staged by Hizbullahis, vigilantes directed by the more militant leading clerics of the regime. Describing a recent assault in which he was badly beaten up while lecturing in Shiraz in June 1995, Sorush recounted his repeated efforts to engage his attackers in debate. "I tried to reason with them. You must always try to reason with such people," he told me, implying a new God-given mission: saving Islamic government and its alleged defenders from their excesses and errors.

Like Turabi and Fadlallah, he, too, is a man of enormous ego. But who else would continue taking such risks? Ultimately, Sorush still considers himself an Islamist who believes in Islamic government, or so he says. But he, like so many other former revolutionaries, has learned through Iran's Islamic experiment that there is no Islamic way to build a car or grow vegetables, any more than there is a single Islamic truth or vision of government that is infallible or just. Sorush's arguments give heart to those who still believe that Islamic government, or a different version of it, can be made to work in Iran. And they also fear that unless the system can reform itself, its many contradictions will cause an implosion, an utter rejection not only of Islamic rule, but of Islam itself.

I have dwelled on these three leaders — Islamists all — not only to highlight their similarities, but also the enormous differences among them. While they share certain personality traits — charisma, a strong ego, a sense of destiny and fatalistic mission, and enormous political pragmatism — their differences are equally striking. Turabi, unlike Fadlallah and Sorush, is a Sunni Arab leader. But while Sorush and Fadlallah may both be Shiites, they are as different as the Iran and Lebanon that produced them. Sorush, who studied in Europe, speaks flawless English and appears utterly at home with Western philosophers from Hegel to the deconstructionists of the late twentieth century. He would hardly be able to identify, much less debate with authority, the ideas of the many Arab-Islamic historical figures who are the heroes and villains of Fadlallah's learned tomes. Other than the need for Islam to prevail, they would probably agree on little in domestic or foreign policy. Fadlallah's obsession with, say, devising a strategy for dealing with Israel, is of little concern to either Turabi, who is focused on consolidating power in impoverished Sudan, or Sorush, intent on changing the nature of Islamic rule inside what was once one of the region's wealthiest oil states.

Their differences also reflect their political circumstances. For while all three are pragmatists determined to remain powerful figures in their societies, their evolution reflects the stage of their respective Islamic experiments. Turabi abandoned democratic and liberal Islam in 1989 in order to seize and now retain power in his strife-torn country. For Fadlallah, evolution meant embracing elections to consolidate and legitimize Hizbullah's political base and prepare for either leaner or more propitious times. For Sorush, political survival has meant turning his back on the failed revolution of 1979 that empowered men like him, ostensibly in the name of saving Islam.

Such differences among leaders of movements that claim to want more or less the same thing should give pause to those fond of grand generalizations about Islamic militancy and its leaders. Despite so many ostensible similarities, differences and diversity prevail.

NOTES

1. Judith Miller, *God Has Ninety-Nine Names: Reporting from a Militant Middle East* (New York, 1996).
2. For more on Turabi, see Gabriel R. Warburg, "Turabi of the Sudan: Soft-Spoken Revolutionary," *Middle Eastern Lectures*, no. 1 (1995): 85-97. *Ed*.
3. On the controversy surrounding Khamenei's claims, see Shaul Bakhash, "Iran: The Crisis of Legitimacy," *Middle Eastern Lectures*, no. 1 (1995): 99-118. *Ed*.

Royals and Revolutionaries
in the Middle East

by P.J. Vatikiotis

P.J. Vatikiotis offered this extemporaneous summation of proceedings at a conference on "Islam, Monarchy and Modernity in the Middle East" at Tel Aviv University.

The post-1918 Arab monarchies which were set up by the British in the Hijaz, Egypt and Iraq, were successors to the Ottoman sultanate. They had the trappings of a throne, of a royal court, yet they were confusing and confused, torn between modernity and tradition. In other words, they were in limbo. And they had the parallel problems introduced by the British, who had erected a rickety scaffolding of constitutional representative government under their tutelage and protection. Why did they remain in limbo? Because they failed to establish the most important requisite of any kind of constitutional monarchy or representative system: a sound secular public order. They rather superimposed monarchy on a lingering culture and tradition, on a society with old conventions. But the failure to produce a secular order is fatal to all who wish to found a modern state with democracy as its base.

Once the protecting power withdrew from the area, the failure to resolve the most vexing problem, that of regime change or succession, led eventually to military rule. Back in 1969, I first described the regimes of the soldiers as non-hereditary monarchies. They introduced or launched republics, a term inappropriate from the outset, because republic is a Latin term from a combination of *res* and *publica*. *Public* entails a corporate personality, but there was no understanding of the public in this region at the time, as distinct simply from the people. Nor was there an understanding of citizenship. Indeed, republic after 1920 merely became a handy term for any regime that was not a monarchy.

Even the present-day Greeks, who have access to a rich political vocabulary, use the same term for republic and democracy, so that when a Greek says "in our democracy," one is not certain whether he is talking about a political system and form of government, or referring to the Republic of Greece. If one considers the Arabic terms *jumhur* or *jumhuriyya*, they are not really synonymous with the New Testament term *to plethos,* nor are they close to the classical term *to koinon* used to refer to the public (or the common and communal), as opposed to the private (and individual).

Dynasticism was replaced in the 1950s and 1960s by what I described as non-hereditary monarchies. In point of fact, they perpetuated autocracy in a new guise. Monarchy, after all, is one-man rule or authority. *Mulk,* kingship, has connotations that evolved with the language, of proprietary rights, ownership. The shift to populist autocracy involved a transfer of title, not an abolition of the proprietary rights of the ruler.

Kings and presidents in the Middle East have had this in common: the drive for hegemonic power, the inability to share power in the formula we know as constitutional monarchy. Consider, for example, the notorious and revealing stand of King Fu'ad of Egypt regarding constitutional government. When the British issued their unilateral declaration of the independence of Egypt and offered the country a constitution, Fu'ad is reported to have complained of British ignorance about his country and the wishes of its people. He could handle his own people, his subjects, who understood only autocratic rule. Fu'ad was not interested in the constitution; when it was drafted and submitted to him, he sent it back demanding greater powers for himself, beyond those of a constitutional monarch.

In Egypt under this constitution, there was always a rivalry for top place between the king and some of his more charismatic "popularly elected" prime ministers or politicians. One of them had to prevail. Such was the rivalry between King Fu'ad and the Wafd party, and even more so between King Faruq and the Wafd. At many points, each side sought to establish popular autocracies in an alliance either with religious elements, or so-called street forces, or both, as the history of the 1930s and 1940s attests. In this contest of attempted autocracies, one of them had to prevail. Whether we are considering monarchy or republic, the tendency is towards the hegemony of power. Rulers tend historically to be hegemonists of power, and that is why one of the contestants or rivals must prevail, since power cannot be shared.

This, too, is why monarchies were abolished. When the Free Officers in Egypt grabbed power by overthrowing the ancien régime in July 1952, they did not know exactly what they were going to do with the institution of monarchy. But the Free Officers were driven to monopolize power largely because they themselves had taken it by force. Today we have many volumes of memoirs by Free Officers, from Abd al-Latif al-Baghdadi to Tharwat Ukasha and others, who describe this pursuit of hegemony in great detail. It might also be added that they were encouraged by the starry-eyed Americans who believed they had found their local hero, Nasser, who would integrate the region under his leadership and control and to their advantage. The Americans were always cost conscious, and in a crude adaptation of their business ethic, sought a cost-efficient policy in the Middle East. Thus they believed they had found their one man, Nasser — which was of course cheaper than having to deal with five or ten men — who in return for their support would promise to maintain a region friendly to American interests.

This pursuit of hegemony, incidentally, has also been the story of the Greek monarchy and its opponents. In 1916-20, sharp differences between the monarch and his prime minister over wartime policy and the orientation in the country's foreign relations amounted to a national feud which created a "National Schism," a terrible split in the country between monarchists and republicans, or between the king's supporters and those of the prime minister. The latter was a very popular, charismatic, but not very scrupulous lawyer from Crete who became prime minister on the back of a military coup d'état in 1909, and who could not countenance sharing the top spot with the king. With the support of the Entente allies, namely Britain and France, he worked assiduously to undermine the position of the monarch until he forced him off the throne and into exile. There was a repetition of this with his young grandson Constantine and his prime minister, Karamanlis. A powerful politician and autocratic personality, Karamanlis was the closest thing to a Greek sultan, who in turn could not countenance sharing the spotlight with the young monarch who ultimately lost his throne and went into exile. I am trying to emphasize a feature of the region, namely, the tendency to the hegemony of power, or to monopolize and personalize power which precludes its being shared; hence the phenomenon of autocracy.

The Salience of Autocracy

Monarchy is often described as institutionalized corruption, but what constitutes a corrupt polity? Is it not also Papandreou's reported "Pink

Palace" with eighteen toilets and three swimming pools in Athens, and the inflated bank accounts of princes, ministers and politicians in most of the states of the region, monarchies and republics alike? One of the best comparisons that I have seen, first published in 1984, and which went through several printings, has been the book by Husayn Mu'nis, *Bashawat wa suber-bashawat* (Pashas and Super-Pashas). The definition of pasha was the chap before 1952 who, in order to become a pasha, had to produce something. But the super-pashas were Nasser's creatures. They produced nothing, they were just influence-peddling middlemen, and overnight they became millionaires.

The harsh autocratic — really arbitrary authoritarian — nature of the so-called republics or non-hereditary monarchies after the British withdrawal, can be illustrated by incidents involving some of my friends and acquaintances. A friend of over forty years, the late critic Louis Awad, was arrested in 1959 along with several others and put in a crowded prison cell pending interrogation. A graduate of Cambridge and Princeton universities, Louis told his fellow-inmates in English: "We must seek to get a writ of habeas corpus." But the officer on duty understood English, grabbed Louis, and began to beat him up rather badly, muttering and screaming: "What habeas corpus? This is how it is here."

Another one, Muhammad Sid Ahmad, a leading journalist and prominent member of the Egyptian Left, was also the nephew of the notorious strongman politician of the 1930s, Isma'il Sidqi Pasha. He was himself the son and grandson of pashas, so he could also be identified as coming from the privileged class of Egypt. He was partially deaf when he was arrested. Along with the other inmates of that prison cell, Sid Ahmad was due to undergo a routine physical examination one morning. The medical officer arrived and began the roll call for that purpose. Sid Ahmad's full name is Muhammad Abbas Sid Ahmad. So when the medical officer read out loud "Muhammad Abbas," he thought he heard the order "fik el-libas!" and so he promptly dropped his pants in preparation for the imminent medical examination. Needless to say, after they were finished with Muhammad, he was almost completely deaf.

The third case is that of Isma'il Sabri Abdallah, who was a member of the Communist Party in Egypt, and who later was director of the National Institute of Planning and at one time minister of planning. His torture at the hands of the military regime left his face badly disfigured. This is what the autocrat Nasser, the great hero of many politicians and social scientists in the West in the 1950s and the 1960s, did to his own people.

If one were to stop and look at the way some Egyptians reacted to this kind of regime terror, one will find that the late playwright and short-story writer Dr. Yusuf Idris protested against the system in a brilliant play he wrote and staged in the National Theater in 1962-63. Called *Al-Farafir*, the play ran for two years before a packed house. It was a subtle attack on the system. Then in 1971 or 1973 Yusuf attended the opening of the circus in Cairo — the opening performance of the season — where he witnessed one of the lions, named Sultan, kill the lion tamer. Yusuf returned immediately to his desk at *Al-Ahram* and wrote one of the most moving and poignant pieces, *Ana Sultan, qanun al-wujud* (I am Sultan, the Law of Being). In symbolic terms, the state, the government was the sultan, the lion, while the Egyptians were the sheep it devoured.

But in my view the most subtle attempt to get back at the regime, to protest against the way it conducted itself with its own people, to high-light the autocracy and what it did, was made by Naguib Mahfouz in his short novel with the ancient pharaonic title *Al-Karnak* (The Temple of Karnak). It is the story of a group of friends who met regularly in a coffee house, when every so often one of them would disappear for months. Before his disappearance the friend was talkative and voluble, but when he reappeared he was totally silent, a minion; in other words, someone who had been to one of the regime's prisons and silenced.

Another instance of what popular or unpopular autocracies do to their own people arises from the story of a former student of mine who is now a respectable university professor. When he was an undergradu-ate at the American University of Beirut, he was for a time secretary of the political bureau of the Arab Nationalist Movement (ANM) led by George Habash before it became the Popular Front for the Liberation of Palestine (PFLP). When many years later I interviewed him for a place for a research degree, I asked him what he wanted to work on. He waffled on something about third world ideology. I ended the interview by sug-gesting he go away and return later with more sensible ideas, and dis-missed him. Years later his wife told me that he had come back from that first interview greatly agitated and told her: "This mad Greek threw me out."

But he did come back and did a very good thesis. He decided to deal with the question of why a particular elite came to power in Egypt in

1919 and not another one. I had sent him to read in the archives. Months later he came to see me and said, "These people I've been reading about, Adli Yeken, Abd al-Khaliq Tharwat and others of their contemporaries, were not really traitors, were they?" When I asked who told him that, he replied: "We were always told that people like them were traitors." But he had discovered they were negotiating with the British on the basis of their particular perception of what the Egyptian national interest at that time was. I encouraged him by mumbling something to the effect that he was learning and would survive the course. Later, when I ventured to ask him about his experiences with the ANM and the Arab states, he retorted without hesitation that having been roughed up by every Arab state police force, he concluded these were all terrorist regimes. What I am trying to underline here is the effect that popular autocracies in the region can have on their people.

Resolve of the Ruler

In understanding autocracies, it is crucial to assess the role of the individual. It was Sir Isaiah Berlin who firmly insisted that subjective choice is important in history and politics. I insist that the choices rulers make are of the utmost importance and relevance to our understanding of the history and politics of the Middle East.

Consider the failures of King Faruq, the subject of a very well-written book by Adel M. Sabit, Faruq's maternal cousin, entitled *A King Betrayed: The Ill-Fated Reign of Farouq of Egypt* (London, 1989). Sabit's book is not an apologia for his cousin, but an interesting, poignant discussion of the unfortunate monarch and his rule, making it clear that with an oriental despot for a father like King Fu'ad, Faruq was doomed — did not have a chance. Contrast this with King Husayn of Jordan. One of the greatest factors in the survival of Jordan was the personal political instinct, acumen and courage of the monarch himself, which helped him defeat his enemies in 1957 and in 1970-71. One cannot overlook or ignore the personality of rulers and the choices they make in considering the survival of their rule.

And it is a failing of would-be revolutionaries to assume that a determined monarch cannot stand up to them successfully. In 1968-69, I dined in the home of a friend in Beirut with many of my old school friends, most of whom I had not seen in twenty-five years. The conversation of the evening centered upon the exploits of our old schoolmate, the late Wadie Haddad, prominent Palestinian revolutionary and aircraft hijacker extraordinaire. Soon it transpired he was advocating — and announcing — that his Palestinian revolutionary organization would take over Jordan. He did so in a typically cavalier fashion, for he had not seriously considered the strength of the opposition to such a venture. Sure enough, weeks later he and his colleague and fellow revolutionary George Habash (they were students in the AUB Medical School together) showed up in Amman. There they began to issue a string of revolutionary proclamations and intemperate announcements, to indulge in guerrilla-type armed clashes, and to blow up foreign airline aircraft. We all know what happened: they provoked the powerful retaliation of the Jordanian state and its armed forces in suppressing them, during the so-called "Black September."

If one looks at the interesting case of the Hashemites in Jordan, one is struck with the title by which people address the king. Very few use *jalalat al-malik* or *jalalatuka*, "Your Majesty." Rather they address him as *sayyidna*, "our master," which is both a religious and tribal style of address. It is really "our chief." And when they address his brother, the crown prince — even though they may have known him for many years — they would never dream of addressing him as anything but *sidi*. These are interesting forms of royal address, especially when contrasted to those in use in Egypt, where *jalala* (majesty) was common but where also the Ottoman expression *effendim* highlights the difference between the two societies in their perception and approach to monarchy. Perhaps too it explains why monarchy failed in Egypt and survived in Jordan.

A charismatic king — even a potential one — is a force to be reckoned with. Is this perhaps why the Greeks two summers ago had all their air force and half their navy chasing the ex-king who was on a family sailing holiday in a yacht along the Greek coast? They were petrified, and that tells one something not only about the ex-king and his family, but about the so-called Republic of Greece which displaced the monarchy. The young crown prince pretender, the eldest son of the ex-king, is smarter still: not only does he have charisma and served as a commissioned officer in the British army, but he also recently married a very rich American woman. Now he is probably perceived by some as even more of a threat to the republic.

Democracy and Secularism

But is not monarchy against our principles? After all, monarchy, we know as a rule, is not an enlightened agency. The "new world order," they tell us, emphasizes democracy and pluralism. The West European proclivity to export political cultures and political norms such as cosmopolitanism, pluralism, and democracy, has certain advantages. But it is also dangerous. There is now, for instance, the mindless notion that if we spend millions of dollars in American and British universities to export democracy, we will be doing well.

Will we? Let us assume that one of the fundamental features of democracy is the vote or elections. What are elections for, when one exports them to the Middle East? Before they can be meaningful, they ought to be held in more open societies — in societies where there is far wider public debate of public issues and where those who are different from the majority are readily tolerated and effectively protected; in societies where there is a consensus on a minimum of common fundamentals, as for example that it is a good thing to have a king in Jordan, as it is a good thing to have a pope in the Vatican. In other words, one can't have the vote when one is not after political change or an alternative government, but actually wants to use elections or exercise the vote in order to abolish the system. I am, therefore, pessimistic about "exporting" democracy to the Middle East, and specifically about busybodies from foundations setting out to "teach democracy." But I am optimistic about the possibility of an indigenous evolution toward more open political systems or regimes, and again perhaps Jordan is a good example.

Then there is the matter of the so-called religious militants, those in Egypt, Algeria, and the Sudan, who insist they are promoting the *hakimiyya* (sovereignty or rule) of God. These are the ones who complain or protest that rule is not Islamic enough and therefore must be opposed and overthrown; or equally in this country, Israel, those who complain that rule or the polity of Israel is not Judaic enough: the people among Muslims and Jews alike who join power and sanctity.

When such militants lose the argument, they turn to violence, and when they speak about injustice and reform they are not Mother Teresa or Francis of Assisi. I have known — and have read about — too many theologies of injustice in history which often led to the darkest, most oppressive of tyrannies. So let us not advise our political masters to "Talk to the moderate militants!" It is currently fashionable among Western students of the Middle East to argue that militant Islamic extremism is a social protest movement. But this, in my view, only betrays and reflects tragic ignorance, based partly on an improper and mistaken borrowing from the Middle Ages in Christian Europe. There is a recurrent phenomenon since the late nineteenth century of violent Muslim reaction to the encroachments of a creeping modernity from the West.

But if we prefer modernity and wish to create a secular political order, how do we uncouple sanctity from power, how do we separate them? That is a problem not only in the neighboring Arab states, but very much a problem here in Israel too. I am surprised that my Israeli academic colleagues discuss the issue of religious militancy, of militant Islam, as if they are talking about a problem on a distant continent or planet when they refer to it in the Arab states. These states, incidentally, are only next door, and their problems with religious militancy are parallel if not similar to those faced by Israel. Religious militancy, extremism and zealotry are a problem shared by the Islamic Arab states and Israel, because at the core of national identity in both societies lies religion. Neither of them so far has constructed a seriously secular public order, or a man-made polity at the center of which is man, not God, a finite political cosmos of human institutions and contrivances, a polity that does not include the promise of salvation.

My late great colleague and friend Elie Kedourie never tired of reminding all who would listen that there is no salvation in politics, and I always added to his aphorism the suggestion that politics is a human device for a passing, mundane, and orderly existence which also tries to keep us from cutting one another's throats. Modernity requires the state to be a political, not an ideological or theological concept. That is what is needed if one wants to be modern and secular. In a modern secular state, land is a territorial and geographical, not a theological, concept. Apocalypse and the fulfillment of prophecies have nothing to do with the state and its mundane politics. As someone who lives in the West and culturally belongs to it for good or ill, I can assure you that the apocalyptic, messianic, militant, religious political game can exact a very high cost in terms of human life.

It was my putative or presumed ancestors, the ancient Greeks (and I insist on the term presumed because I cannot claim any genealogical link, only a linguistic and cultural affinity and inheritance, a legacy of continuity) who expelled the gods from their mundane human affairs. It is the only way for man to be responsible for his political decisions in the public domain, and not shift the responsibility onto the shoulders of a deity, be it God, Allah, or Adonai. For the lingering medieval, apocalyptic, messianic manifestations of politics in the Middle East, I shall borrow Albert Camus's phrase to the effect that no amount of scientific explanation and demonstration, or ideological hocus pocus, can convince me that this world, let alone the next, is mine.

"System" Breakdown in the Middle East?

by Yezid Sayigh

Over a decade ago ago, the historian L. Carl Brown of Princeton University wrote a book in which he described the Middle East as the most penetrated international sub-system in international relations today. This was the year before Gorbachev came to power in the Soviet Union, and several years before the end of the cold war.

Viewing the Middle East ten years later, there is a temptation to ask if any semblance of a Middle East system survives at all. Is the Middle East still really penetrated, is it even a distinct regional system with its own identifiable and unique patterns? Or are the individual states and subregional groupings of states within the Middle East in the process of being integrated separately, and to unequal degrees, within a wider international system, itself characterized by growing anarchy, multipolarity, and intensifying economic competition?

I am posing these questions in a somewhat exaggerated form, but they are pertinent to understanding the emerging structure of power and politics in the Middle East. Answering them might suggest the dynamics that will govern regional politics in the near future. I will enquire first into the patterns of interstate relations, then the prospects for regional organization, and finally the factors that I believe will determine the nature of regional politics.

In doing so, I will borrow the concepts of "system" and "order" from the terminology of international relations. Different people in different disciplines use these concepts quite differently, so I should stress that that I use "system" in the international relations sense to mean a group of bodies, parties or actors that over time have a repeated or iterated pattern of interaction, whether strategic, economic, or social. Moreover, these bodies or actors within a system may come together and agree to abide by certain rules. Where there is formality in their interactions, then we may speak of an "order," which may or may not be embodied in formal institutions. So when I speak of a "system," I refer only to very broad interaction. This interaction may still be anarchic. It may rest on balance of power politics, but it is not necessarily defined by agreed terms, norms, and values.

On that basis, I distinguish between two separate systems that have operated in the Middle East in the past, and certainly since 1945. There is the Arab state system, or the system of Arab states. In 1945, Arab states came together to create a formal order, the League of Arab States. The Arab state system thus has the additional defining feature of order.

However, the Arab order obviously does not include Israel and Iran. Both countries are nonetheless part of the Middle East and its strategic system. Therefore, I distinguish between the Arab state system and the Middle East strategic system. This wider system includes all the states in the region, because they have tended to have very heavy patterns of interaction with their neighbors. However, because of the lack of diplomatic recognition or the acknowledgement of their legitimacy by their neighbors, Iran and Israel (and particularly Israel) have not become a part of the region's state system.

The Rise and Fall of the Arab System

With these distinctions in mind, allow me to look first at the Arab state system and identify some of the patterns of the past and changes since the end of the cold war. The Arab state system has been marked by the attempt to build order. Despite common belief, the League of Arab States was not constructed in order to achieve Arab union. It was based on the principle of the sovereignty and territorial integrity of its member states. The member states acknowledged that they would remain separate, not united. In fact, it was only because these principles were endorsed in the foundation of the League of Arab States that it could come into being at all. Although the League established a number of specialized bodies to deal with collective defense, economics, education, industrial and technical cooperation, the League's various decisions and resolutions were not binding upon its members. Nor were they enforceable.

The League of Arab States mediated in inter-Arab politics, especially through its stronger members. Egypt's mediating role under Nasser in the late 1960s, in Jordan and Lebanon, is one example. Saudi Arabia in the 1970s used its financial leverage to mediate. In these cases, the League of Arab States could mediate because of the activism of its stronger members. But the League itself was weak, and it failed to play the more decisive role of arbiter. It lacked mechanisms and institutions that were essential to conflict resolution and arbitration, as we all saw so clearly in 1990.

The point I wish to make is that the League of Arab States as an order lacked the institutions and mechanisms for system maintenance. And because it could not move forward at any level — strategic, political, economic, or social — the opposite occurred. At the point where it stopped, it could only decline, even degenerate.

The other aspect I wish to stress is that both the League of Arab States and the Arab state system were dominated by balance of power politics. Relations between the states were determined by the balance of power between them, or their ability to find other powerful allies within their state system, or even to find powerful allies altogether outside the Middle East, especially a superpower patron. Balancing politics predominated throughout the Arab system, despite the existence of an order with nominal shared principles. Moreover, the patterns of global competition, of U.S.-Soviet rivalry, superimposed themselves on local balancing politics, deepening divisions and exacerbating tensions. Any individual Arab state (indeed any individual Middle East state) could increase its margin for autonomous action within the region by securing local or global allies. This encouraged positionality: the assessment by each state or government of the position it occupied within the wider Arab state system, and the measurement of its gains or losses against the gains or losses of any of its partners or rivals within the system. This in turn encouraged the relative gains approach: a calculation of who stood to make more, who to make less, from any given action.

Based on what I have just said, one might question whether an Arab order ever existed at all. It is a fair question, and a difficult one to answer. But certainly by 1990, the failures and shortcomings of the order as it existed had become very evident. Neither the League of Arab States nor any grouping of Arab states had managed to deal effectively with strife in Lebanon in the mid-1970s, the Iran-Iraq war, the crisis in the Horn of Africa, the Western Sahara conflict, or Iraqi-Kuwaiti tensions and the Iraqi invasion of Kuwait.

Now, to move from the Arab state system to the absent partners, if you like: Israel and Iran, both members of the Middle East strategic system. The Arab rivalry with Israel and Iran was perhaps the main point of entry for cold war politics throughout the last four or five decades. If we look back at the impact of the cold war on the Middle East, it was most evident along the Arab-Israeli divide and the Iraqi-Iranian (or Gulf-Iranian) divide. What characterized relations between Israel and its neighbors, and Iran and its neighbors, was the iteration, in other words the repeated pattern and interaction, at the strategic level. We may call the Middle East a strategic system precisely because there was so little interaction with Israel and Iran at any other level, most notably the political. Iran, of course, did enjoy formal diplomatic relations with the Arab states, but there was little real political interaction beyond that. There was minimal economic interaction and, until the mid-1970s, little coordination over oil. The same could be said several times over with respect to Israel, since it enjoyed no diplomatic relations with Arab states at all. The locus of interaction was military and strategic; relations were defined by mutual distrust, delegitimization and conflict.

Among Arab states, rivals would compete by invoking a common cause such as Palestine, or appealing to each other's populations in attempts at subversion. But this logic could not work in Arab-Iranian or Arab-Israeli relations. There was no real scope for an appeal from one side to the other side's population. However, governments could use nationalism and national conflict to mobilize their own home fronts, to justify authoritarian rule, and to legitimize militarization and statist economic policies.

This was the picture until 1990. Since the end of the cold war, and the Gulf war that immediately followed, two main developments have affected the Arab state system. One is the acceleration of the Arab-Israeli peace process. An Arab-Israeli peace means that Israel is in the process of becoming a full member of a Middle East state system, not just the strategic system. It is part of the system not only because it interacts militarily and strategically with neighbors in cases of conflict. Israel now recognizes and is recognized by its neighbors, and therefore is able to interact with them at other levels. The extent of economic and commercial interaction is not the point here. The point is that dealing with Israel, being a partner with Israel, is no longer sufficient grounds for one Arab state to exclude another Arab state from the Arab state system, as occurred with Egypt at the end of the 1970s. This means is that Israel is becoming part of a larger state system.

The Dissolving Middle East

But which state system? Is the Middle East strategic system simply becoming a state system? Are the two now synonymous? I would argue that the Middle East strategic system is dissolving or fragmenting, that it is turning into something new. The Arab state system is also in the process of restructuring, fragmentation, maybe even dissolution. So we have a blurring of lines between the two, and each within itself is changing and dividing.

Let us look for a moment at what is happening on the Arab side. Peace with Israel, even if it has not yet included Syria and Lebanon, has removed a main driving force behind balance of power or balancing politics on the Arab side. If Palestine in the past was used by various Arab governments to outbid each other — to say we are more militant, more nationalist, than thou — this card can no longer be played. The ability of Arab governments to use the Palestine issue to mobilize resources, whether from their local population, from other Arabs who happen to be richer, or from a superpower patron, is also diminished. With the end of the cold war, the Soviet patron is gone, and the U.S. and other Western nations need no longer pay the same high strategic rents (or, if you prefer, bribes) they paid in the past. States like Syria and Egypt cannot now extract external assistance for military budgets from the oil-rich states. Furthermore, the ability of Arab governments to use the Palestine issue in their internal politics and in maintaining their political control has been undermined. The balancing politics that defined relations between Arab states has lost a major component. There will no doubt be competition between certain Arab states over the rewards of peace. But this competition generally takes a milder form; it does not surface as political subversion, as sabotage attacks between Arab capitals.

If Israel is becoming a member of the system, then conceivably balancing politics will now start to cut across the Arab-Israeli divide. We may find Israel and various Arab partners balancing against other Arab or Middle Eastern parties. If subregional groupings emerge, along the lines of the Gulf Cooperation Council, the Arab-Maghrib Union or some new Mashriq-Levantine association, Israel will no longer be excluded. It will be difficult for any new group of Arab states, except for the League of Arab States itself, to coalesce without Israel, and were it to do so, it would risk swift irrelevance. So at least in Arab functional groupings — groupings set up to deal with the environment, collective security, economic reconstruction — we will find Israel and at least some Arab states sitting together. Furthermore, peace with Israel specifically is important for several Arab states, if only because these Arab states are looking to the West and the U.S. for increased rewards, interaction, cooperation, trade, and aid. For many Arabs, peace with Israel above all offers the prospect of better relations with America.

This takes me to the second main development since the end of the cold war and the Gulf war: the reorientation of the strategic system, as the various members of the system reorient themselves to the new global balance. No doubt there will be variations, in some cases very significant, in how different states restructure their patterns of external relations, adjust their defense and foreign policy posture, and restructure internally. Nonetheless, there is a broad pattern leading to a fragmentation of the Middle East system.

What do I mean by this? The Gulf war very demonstrably divided the Arab states. It struck any remaining notion of pan-Arabism a deadly blow. And if nothing else, it revealed the paralysis of the League of Arab States. The Gulf war has also left us with the dominant, visible and direct U.S. role in the Gulf, and a preeminent role in the rest of the region. With this comes the policy of containment of Iraq and Iran — a unique situation in which the U.S. plays the leading role both politically and militarily. The containment of Iran and Iraq, with the extension of the U.S. strategic umbrella to the rest of the Gulf, means a suspension of the preexisting strategic sub-system within the Gulf. That is, the past pattern of strategic interactions among the states of the southern Gulf, Iraq and Iran — a pattern of balancing politics and courting local allies — has been suspended. It does not operate as before, because Iran and Iraq effectively have been neutralized. In the meantime, the Maghrib is increasingly concerned with its own problems, revolving around trade, aid and migration to Europe. The result is a disarticulation of the wider Middle East strategic system, if one ever existed.

The Arab state system is dissolving, the Middle East strategic system is being restructured. Does this mean that system behavior — anarchic relations, balancing politics — has disappeared entirely? Certainly, the strategic component that defined the system has weakened. Since conflict in the Gulf and between Arabs and Israel has been suspended, so inevitably the strategic dimension and its impact have weakened. Balancing politics is weakened too, if only because the Arab states that used those conflicts in order to mobilize resources, maintain authoritarian rule, and maintain external alliances can no longer do so. If this is the case, does a regional system have some other basis of existence? Is there anything else besides strategic, economic, political, and social relations? Is there anything else that involves constant, repeated and heavy interaction between states?

Here let me introduce the idea of the balance of interest. The notion first emerged in the last days of the Soviet Union, when Gorbachev started to speak in terms of the mutuality of security, resting on a balance of interest, not a balance of power. Since the acceleration of the Arab-Israeli peace process, balance of interest has also become a buzzword when talking about the Middle East. This is a balance by which we all seek our mutual interests and allow each other to live, instead of viewing each other in hard political and strategic terms. The idea is that states can recognize each other's interests, and are willing to exchange interests as well, even to the extent of creating formal organizations for regional security and regional cooperation. That is, they may actually institutionalize their balance of interest.

I see two opposing dynamics here. Certainly there is the dynamic of the balance of interest, which has some basis in material reality. However, I see a number of other patterns and trends that are powerful and may not give way to the balance of interest and its logic.

One is structural. For all Middle Eastern countries, economic, commercial, strategic, political, and military links to outside powers are of paramount importance. When it comes to the flow of arms, strategic relations and protection, aid, credit, and trade, there is not one Middle Eastern country (with the possible exception today of Iran) which does not have the vast bulk of its relations with a non-Middle Eastern power. To give a simple example, external trade between Arab states accounts for 7 or 8 percent of total Arab trade. In other words, over 90 percent of the total external trade of Arab states is with non-Arab countries. What basis is there then for a balance of interest between them in the realm of economic cooperation and development? They now cooperate economically with distant and non-Arab economies. In a scenario of peace, the potential rewards also lie in economic relations outside the Middle East.

Furthermore, there is a high degree of similarity in the economic capabilities and resources of many Arab states. Most of them produce identical types of light industrial products. A lot of them produce oil, others produce agricultural goods. They tend to operate and to compete in the same space. That could lead to conflict and tension. Or it could lead simply to further detachment, since they don't have much ground for cooperation in the first place. For now, the more crucial interaction takes place in their relations with non-Arab powers: the West, the U.S., and Israel.

Indeed, I see a situation where there is competition not between many Arab states for overall Arab primacy, but between pairs of states for primacy in relations with non-Arab partners. Such competition takes place between Syria and Lebanon, Jordan and the Palestinians, Egypt and Jordan, all in relation to Israel. If there is any reorienting or restructuring of the patterns of relations among these Arab parties, it relates to Israel in some way, or it is being measured in terms of the relationship with Israel, rather than in terms of coordination with each other. Each country is making its own calculation in relation to Israel.

In short, we have here a classic case of the relative gains syndrome. Each Arab party now asks itself: "Who is getting more out of this deal, me or some other Arab?" After the signing of the Oslo accords between the PLO and Israel, the Egyptian and Jordanian press became preoccupied with the question of which Arabs stood to get more out of a Palestinian-Israeli economic accord. Did Egypt stand to benefit more, and would it lean on the Palestinians to make sure that the economic accord strengthened the Egyptian position? Did Jordan stand to lose to Egypt, and would it lean also on the Palestinians, or simply cut its own deal?

And so we find that Israel, at least in this area of the Arab world, holds the key. There is no multilateral collective agency that deals with economic, environmental or security issues. Rather we have a single actor, Israel, signing a series of bilateral deals with each Arab party, each of which separately calculates its losses and gains. The Arab parties do not coordinate; to the contrary, they compete.

What are the implications for regional security and cooperation? To my mind, they are not good. There isn't a strong urge to seek regional organization, promote collective agencies, and build formal institutions, either because there are more gains to be achieved from dealing with the outside world, or more gains to be achieved from dealing bilaterally with Israel in a competitive way.

Within this type of situation, those states that are stronger in terms of organizational and economic capability can dominate the terms of exchange and distribution of benefits. The small states might seek allies and the umbrella of some larger state. The new system, or that part of the system within the Arab-Israeli sphere, is being restructured and reoriented, but under a specific balance of power, as in the Gulf. It is based upon a suspension of the strategic conflict. There is a new rule of the game at the strategic level: thou shalt not wage war. Each state has to secure its own position bereft of the tools of military coercion.

Now that of course begs the question: what happens if there is some major change, either within one of the states of this system or outside it? What happens, for instance, if dual containment comes undone in the Gulf? What happens when the embargo of Iraq is finally lifted, as one day it will be? We might wind up with three Iraqs; we might have a single Iraq. It might be a totally demilitarized Iraq or it might be a powerful Iraq. Whatever the outcome, it will affect all the other players.

In the event of such a change, no one can predict what pattern will emerge. Will the region move back to classic balancing politics? Will we go once again to an anarchic system in which the stronger states — Israel, perhaps Jordan and Saudi Arabia, each in its own theater — dominate, not through crude power but through their superior organizational capacity and ability to mobilize and generate resources? Or do we move somewhere else? At present, there exists a balance of interest, but it is ephemeral and transitional, the result of the suspension of a specific strategic configuration. Each party is looking out for its own interest, measuring its own gains and losses and behaving accordingly within the limits of its own capabilities, its own assets, its own external alliances. But this is a transitional phase, likely to yield to something different.

Factor X: Domestic Crisis

A crucial factor for that future change will be domestic. There is a deep economic, social, political and structural crisis throughout the Middle East, especially in the Arab states. Israel aside, the rest of the Middle East, including Iran, is in a structural crisis. The existing structures of state in most Middle East countries are no longer able to cope with the demands of growing populations, the shortage of housing, the need for jobs, the demands for education, health care, clean water. When a state *structure* is incapable of providing those basic entitlements and needs, the crisis is no longer one of policy, but runs deeper. It is structural partly because it is built into the economic and political systems that have emerged since independence in Arab states.

To give you a quick idea of population growth, for instance, the current population of the Arab states is estimated at about 200 million. Within about ten or fifteen years, it will reach 300 million, then 450 million by the year 2025. To provide jobs for the people who are already employable today means an increase of 45 percent in available jobs over the next fifteen years, 60 percent if we count everyone who is under twenty. Where are those jobs going to come from?

The decline of oil revenues, and of the real value of oil — in real terms the price of oil today hovers around where it stood in 1970, before the oil price boom — has vast implications, not only for the oil-rich states but for all the states in the region that benefit, directly or indirectly, from the flow of oil, petrodollars, and remittances of expatriate labor. The decline of rent — strategic rent, oil rent — also affects the nature of political and social control. Most Middle East governments have based their social and political control on the ability to extract rent and to provide some form of subsidized welfare. Whether it is Ba'thist single-party rule, or the FLN in Algeria, or the monarchical system of Saudi Arabia, we see the same pattern of statist economic policies, implemented either through official central economic planning, or heavy subsidies, or a controlled relationship between the private sector and the public sector, as in Egypt.

This sort of crisis is not one that easily can be resolved by reform. Rigid authoritarian political structures will find it extremely difficult to cope. They can tinker with reform, they can modify and ameliorate. But they cannot undertake the restructuring that will be required to deal with a crisis of this scale, and in attempting to do so they may unleash political, social and economic problems that they will not be able to control.

In some countries the ability of governments to cope, to manage, to extend, to delay, to postpone, will be greater than in other countries, because they have more oil under the ground, or have smaller populations, or embarked on some liberalization earlier, in the 1980s or 1970s. Other countries will be unable to cope, and I think the example of Algeria is an omen: a state structure that simply could not cope even with the burdens of its own population.

This may mean more regional conflict in some cases, but I would argue that the pattern will be predominantly one of internalized conflict. It is easy to look at Islam as a sweeping region-wide phenomenon. Certainly Islam is on the rise and will continue to be on the rise, if only because in many societies, existing political systems and structures no longer offer a channel of incorporation for a large part of the population that is poor but educated, and that can identify and articulate its discontent. But this Islam, despite the surface appearance of being a trans-state phenomenon, is in fact locally rooted. Islamism in Algeria is an Algerian phenomenon. Islamism in Egypt is basically an Egyptian phenomenon.

The patterns of conflict, crisis, even collapse, will not be the consequences of subversion from outside, but will be internal.

In this situation, the coherence of an interstate system, in which countries interact with each other extensively, in conflict or in harmony, is again weakened. The further each state is challenged internally by its structural problems, the less it is able to conduct active interstate relations or embark on foreign adventures and interventions. We are used to thinking that a society in crisis or revolution, whether it is Iran after 1979 or the Bolsheviks after 1917, embarks on a foreign policy of adventurism. That has been true in some cases, but in societies where the resources are far more limited, this is far less likely.

We may end up with a system in which some states remain more or less able to operate cohesively and coherently, to undertake certain reforms, to formulate economic, social, and some foreign policy, and to enter into contractual arrangements with other partners within the system and outside it. But there will be other states — Somalia, possibly Algeria and Sudan, conceivably Iraq if it breaks up — that can no longer function in the ways to which we and they are accustomed. They will not operate cohesively and coherently as states. In that case, we may have a system in which some states enjoy real sovereignty — positive sovereignty — and some states only exist through what is known as negative sovereignty. They persist because other states continue to recognize Algeria or Somalia or the Sudan, but how much do they exist as states that are able to organize, mobilize, deter, and defend? And all this is taking place at a time of continuing global transition, when states that are not global powers are less able and willing to intervene effectively, to offer aid, to assist foreign societies and economies in crisis.

Falling Expectations

So to conclude, what are we left with? First, the peace dividend we have all hoped for will not meet expectations, at least in the short term. Peace is very important: I am not saying that peace cannot make an important and significant change in our lives. It has already started to alter the pattern of interstate relations in our region fundamentally and irreversibly. However, in terms of our ability to divert resources from military into economic uses and to restructure societies accordingly, the peace dividend will be slow in coming. It will be very modest, in a few cases even negative. There will be countries that must initially invest even more in their security, to deal with internal conflict that emerges as a result of this reorientation.

The dividend can increase only if states in the region are able to achieve more regional cooperation and construct multilateral collective agencies. However, the tendency of states will be to operate bilaterally rather than multilaterally or collectively. This is especially true of the poorer countries that already lack resources and face population explosions. Paradoxically, the states that stand to gain the most from cooperation might be those that actually feel they cannot afford to cooperate, and that they must first defend their own narrow interest in the short term.

For Israel, the prospects for economic prosperity from peace are, I believe, grossly exaggerated. We are likely to find that what Israel has to offer in the way of technology, know-how, and organizational capability, is on offer from other competitors around the world, at cheaper prices. Arab states already have traditional trading partners all around the world, and Arab entrepreneurs as well as Arab governments' contracting agents know where to look in South Korea, Japan, the U.S., and Western Europe. It is not clear that Israel has a comparative advantage here.

As for Arab economies, they do not yet offer a particularly attractive target for foreign direct investment. Around the world, most of the foreign direct investment still flows to where it has been flowing for the last decade or two: East Asia, parts of Latin America, the U.S., and Western Europe. Eastern Europe is another competitor for capital. The reason investors have shunned the Arab world is not only conflict, and investment will not begin to flow simply because there is peace. Foreign investors have avoided the area in the past because most of the economies in the region do not have adequate legislative and administrative structures. The level of scientific and technological development, and skills among the labor force in a number of countries, are too low to attract the sort of investment that will spur growth. This has to be factored into our idea of how states will relate to each other, and whether they will be able to extricate themselves from the crisis that faces them.

So the Middle East system faces disarticulation, and this is perhaps even true of its component parts. The domestic dimension is one that deserves far more serious consideration by those powers around the globe that consider themselves the makers of the world agenda and the architects of global security.

Reflections on Islamic Historiography

by Bernard Lewis

Consider the word *history*. It comes from a Greek verb meaning to learn by asking questions — a good way to learn, I think we would all agree. It has the further meaning of inquiring into a subject, and then the derived meaning of narrating what one has learnt by asking questions and inquiring.

Historia developed to mean the relating of a narrative. This may be of events which actually happened or are purported to have happened, or of which the narrator frankly admits himself to be the inventor. In English, we have a bifurcation of this idea of narrative into two kinds: history and story. French uses *histoire* in both senses, while German uses *Geschichte* — a different word from a different root, but still combining these two meanings from the Greek.

The same word, the same root, has found its way into Arabic too, but with a dramatic shift of meaning. The Arabic term is *ustura*. It too derives from the Greek *historia,* but in Arabic, it has the meaning of a tall story. *Ustura* is a fable, a myth, a patently invented tale, and it is interesting that this same term, by what route or channel I do not know, should have suffered so complete a change of meaning in Arabic. It is not that the Arabs, from the earliest times, were not interested in history, but they use a different term to designate it. This is the term *tarikh,* which is used not only in Arabic but, as far as I know, in virtually every other Muslim language.

Now *historia,* as I mentioned earlier, means to learn by inquiry; *tarikh* comes from an old Semitic word meaning the moon. It means, in other words, dating: a system of dating by natural phenomena, and it reflects the concern to establish a precise and accurate chronology. *Tarikh* means, in the modern American idiom, to tell it like it was, or, in the more elegant phrase of von Ranke, "wie es eigentlich gewesen ist." This reflects a profound concern, from the very beginnings of Islamic historiography, to establish a sequence of events, to find out and relate what happened, precisely and accurately. I propose to consider how this was done, in what ways, for what purposes and to what effect.

Attitudes towards the Past

It may be useful to begin by underlining the difference between what
one might call historical and ahistorical societies. There are some civilizations that have reached a high level of material, moral and intellectual
culture without being interested in the past. The outstanding example is
Hindu India, that is, India before the advent of Islam where, despite a
very advanced culture in almost every field of human endeavor, people
displayed no interest worth speaking of in their own past. What little we
know of the history of pre-Islamic India derives either from the spade or
from foreign or later texts. Another example of an ahistorical culture is
that of post-exilic Judaism. There is a marked change from the pre-exilic
concern with history to the post-exilic neglect of history. The Greeks
were very interested in what we would call contemporary history, the
chronicling of the here and now. But there is very little Greek writing
about times that, for them, were ancient. The Romans were rather more
interested in ancient history, principally their own.

All this is by way of background, to set the scene for a study of Islamic
historiography. The first thing that strikes us, looking at the historical
literature of the Islamic world, is its immense richness and variety, as
contrasted even with other history-writing civilizations. It has been cal-
culated that the historical literature of medieval Islam is far greater in
bulk, just in Arabic, than the literatures of medieval eastern and western
Christendom in Latin, Greek and all the vernaculars combined. Islam,
from the very beginning, has attached enormous importance to history.
Indeed, in many parts of the world, reliable history begins with the advent of Islam.

The first kind of historical writing to appear in Islam is that which we
might call heroic: saga, epic, narratives of battles, stories of heroes, the
old Arabian stories known as the *Ayyam al-Arab* (Days of the Arabs)
which tell of the great battles of pre-Islamic Arabia. (Reading the *Ayyam
al-Arab*, I am irresistibly reminded of American football: there is the same
element of sport, and one has the impression that the battles recorded
in the *Ayyam al-Arab* were only slightly more dangerous to life and limb
than American football.) This type of saga literature develops into the
maghazi, the tales of raids which become tales of conquests, the *futuh*,
and form an important component of the traditional biography of the
Prophet who, in addition to being the Prophet, was also an Arab hero in
the traditional style.

This type of saga historiography is most important in the early period. It includes the saga of the Prophet himself, of his Companions, of those immensely successful wars which brought vast territories into the realm of Islam and subject to the rule of the Islamic state. But saga historiography doesn't end there; it continues into much later times, in the form of historical narrative that is halfway between chronicle and epic. Usually it centers around the career and achievements of some heroic figure, particularly in the jihad, the holy war for Islam. Thus, we have several Arabic biographies of Saladin, most notably the work by Imad al-Din, who combines Saladin's biography with his own autobiography, and whose frequent use of rhymed prose and heroic narrative qualifies his work as semi-epic literature. As a later example, I would mention the Ottoman accounts of the Hungarian wars of Suleyman the Magnificent, where the Ottoman historian Kemalpashazade again uses the same kind of literary style — part chronicle, part heroic poetry — to describe the achievements of his hero.

What is the purpose of this heroic literature? It is meant to stimulate, arouse, encourage, stiffen the sinews and summon up the blood, in Shakespeare's phrase. It also has some other purposes which become more important in later times. For want of a better term, I would call this purpose PR, public relations. This becomes almost formalized and certainly becomes a profession. Historical PR comes in a number of forms. The most universal is the poem. Nowadays, rulers employ public relations advisers or consultants. In classical Islamic times, they employed poets. The old histories of literature tell many stories of vast sums being paid by rulers to poets. Normally these were not expressions of literary appreciation, but were payments for services rendered. In a society where there are no mass media, radio, television, or newspapers, there are two ways by which the ruler can address the mass of his subjects: poetry and inscriptions. Inscriptions are there for whoever can read them, or have them read to him, and they proclaim the ruler's greatness, his achievements, and other things he would have his subjects believe about him. But the poet serves the same purpose rather more effectively, producing memorable and easily memorized verses lauding the greatness of his master. A good deal of classical poetry is PR: poems written in praise or eulogy, usually for a political or military chief. There is also negative PR, known as satire.

Rather more formal is the victory letter, a custom going back to remote antiquity, and very much developed in Ottoman times in the *fathname*. When an Ottoman sultan won a battle, the practice was to hire a historian who would then write it up in suitably grandiloquent language. This *fathname* would then be sent to other Muslim rulers, to say "Look what I've done." After the battle of Varna in 1444, when the Ottoman sultan vanquished the Crusaders and captured a considerable number of Western knights, he sent them, in their plumes and feathers, all the way from Turkey to Afghanistan and back, with the *fathname* accompanying them.

Another major type of historical writing is that which is devoted to the collection, establishment and recording of precedents. The historian in these instances functions as the compiler of a casebook. This is needed for a variety of reasons, and there are several different kinds of historical writing that are collections of precedents. One type, predominant in the earlier period, is what one might call the Sunna approach, the *hadith* narratives concerning the actions and utterances of the Prophet, followed by narratives of the doings and sayings of the Companions of the Prophet and the early rulers of Islam. The purpose of these was to establish rules of procedure: the Prophet said or did this, therefore this is right and is an example which should be followed. These are what modern lawyers call casebooks, and they pose two problems: how to treat history as law, and how to treat law as history.

One consequence of this desire to collect precedents and examples from the sanctified figures of the past is an almost obsessive concern with accuracy. If your purpose in history is to find out the manifestation of God's will — and from a Muslim point of view, Sunna is no less than that — it is obviously extremely important to get it right. From an early time, there are not only variant versions but even contradictory versions of the same event; hence the development, by early Muslim historians, of a very sophisticated science of source criticism, a comparative method far in advance of anything known in the world until that time. Modern scholarship has not always agreed with the methods used, but the information provided, sometimes perhaps half a dozen different versions of the same event, all laboriously tabulated, each supported by a chain of narrators attesting to its origins and its authenticity — all this provides a great wealth of material for the modern scholar.

The Sunna approach to history is not the only one concerned with precedent; there is another which we might call *adab*, using a different word that has a meaning similar to Sunna. *Adab* literature develops more in the Abbasid period and after, and its producers and consumers are not primarily men of religion but are rather "men of the pen," civil servants. A great deal of classical Arabic prose literature is written by civil servants for civil servants, to meet the needs of the civil service. These too are collections of precedents set by wise rulers and competent officials. There are also stories about unwise rulers and incompetent officials: one needs negative as well as positive examples. In this school of historical writing, accuracy — getting it right, what actually happened, the actual deeds done and words spoken — matters less than persuasive, convincing and elegant expression, raising all the problems of history as literature and literature as history.

These are the main types of history as precedent in Islamic historical literature. There is another type, relatively less important: biographical literature. Some of the biographical literature is an offshoot of the earlier *hadith-khabar* type: it becomes necessary to establish biographies in order to verify the reliability of narrators and thus the authenticity of the texts which they narrate. Apart from that, biography takes two principal forms: martyrology and hagiography. Both of these are outside the Sunni mainstream of historical writing. Martyrology is Shiite, hagiography is primarily Sufi. From the point of view of the Shia, history does not have that central religious importance that it has for Sunnis, because from the Shiite point of view, with the murder of the Caliph Ali and the withdrawal of his son and successor, history took a wrong turn. After that, history can teach us nothing; it is a long saga of crimes, misdeeds and oppressions. This gives an entirely different quality to Shiite historiography from that of the Sunnis. It also produces that distinctively Shiite brand of historical writing: martyrologies, the record of those who were killed among the descendants of Abu Talib. As for the Sufis, they collect saints, and we have quite a number of collections of Sufi holy men.

Apart from these specialized varieties, biography — which is so important in some other historiographic traditions — is rather limited in the Islamic world. We have great numbers of biographical dictionaries, and I suspect that it was in the Islamic world that the biographical dictionary was invented. But the full-length individual biography is extraordinarily rare, and even the biographical dictionaries are mostly limited. Most were written by scholars and literati, collecting the biographies of scholars and literati, for a readership consisting largely of scholars and literati.

We do not find, as we find in some other societies, notably in Europe, biographies of monarchs. It is extraordinary that, with very few exceptions, even the most famous and active rulers of the Islamic world are not the subjects of individual full-length biographies. I mentioned Saladin before as one of the very few examples. It would be difficult to add many more. There is no real biography of any Abbasid caliph; there are only relevant sections of general histories. One possible explanation that comes to mind is the structure of the Muslim family, which makes it more difficult to achieve the kind of personal knowledge that biographers need. The biographer of an English or French monarch would know things about the monarch's mother, his upbringing, his early life, which for most Muslim rulers are simply unknowable. This information is unavailable even for Ottoman sultans, almost to the end of their dynasty, and that does make biography difficult.

What then is the subject matter of Muslim historiography? Here again we find striking contrasts between the Islamic and the medieval and later European approach. In the Islamic world, we do not find histories of nations. There is no history of the Arabs and no history of the Turks, very remarkable omissions. We do not find many histories of countries, and when we do, it is really city history. A history of Egypt usually means a history of Cairo; a history of Syria, *Sham,* usually means a history of Damascus. One will find local histories of a city and a province, mostly biographical, but no histories of countries in the sense that, further west, people were writing the history of England and the history of France. What we have is universal history, which of course for Muslims means Islamic history, sub-divided into dynastic histories, and to some extent regional histories, but only of the very large regions. (There are for example histories of Muslim Spain and Central Asia.)

Muslim Historiography and the "Other"

How does Muslim historiography look at the history of other peoples, countries, nations, religions? In the civilizations that preceded Islam, there was an almost total lack of interest in the "Other." The Greeks were not particularly interested in other people's history. There were books written about other civilizations, but they were compiled mainly by writers coming from those civilizations, such as the Babylonian Berossos on Babylon and the Egyptian Manetho on Egypt. It is surely significant that these books have not survived, but are known only from quotations. The

Romans show a similar lack of concern with outsiders. The Byzantines do devote some attention to the history of other cultures, and particularly to that of their Islamic neighbor. But much of what the Byzantines write about Islam is in the nature of intelligence reports submitted to the Byzantine administration.

Muslim historiographical horizons did not extend much further. Some foreign history did find its way into the Islamic historiographic tradition, as it was needed by way of background. The Qur'an itself contains elements of earlier history. It deals with the prophets before Muhammad, and with various places and peoples of earlier times. Within the Islamic historiographic tradition it was permissible, indeed necessary, to include pre-Islamic material insofar as this was needed to interpret the Qur'an. For this purpose, we find elements of biblical, Greek and Roman history which became part of the Muslim historiographic tradition. But these amount to very little, and one is astonished by the extent to which the pre-Islamic past was forgotten and obliterated after the conversion of the central lands to the Islamic faith. Indeed, when the Persians began a kind of Persian national renascence in the ninth and still more in the tenth centuries, and tried to recover the history of the fairly recent glories of ancient Iran, they were not really able to do so. Much of the Iranian history that appears at that time is old Persian myth and saga rather than history. Firdawsi's famous *Shahname*, the Book of Kings, is not the real history of ancient Iran, but an entirely mythical saga.

Most astonishing is that the name of Cyrus was unknown in Muslim Iran until the last years of the nineteenth century, when it first became known through Persian translations of a French novel dealing with Cyrus, and some other writings dealing with ancient history. It was recovered through France, where it had been retrieved from the two surviving participants in the history of the ancient Middle East, the Greeks and the Jews.

Of course, one needed to know something about the enemy; it is always useful to have information about the current or prospective adversary whom one is likely to encounter on the battlefield or in the marketplace. But even here we find surprisingly little concern or interest. Crusade versus jihad — the great debate, as Gibbon called it, between Christendom and Islam — exemplifies this lack of interest in the "Other." Jihad was a holy war; the Crusade was a limited and belated Christian response to the jihad, but it extended over a vast area from Spain through southern Italy and Sicily to the Levant. Crusaders and Muslims confronted each other for several centuries in almost total ignorance of each other. The Crusaders show a remarkable lack of curiosity concerning their adversaries, and the Muslims show an even greater lack of curiosity concerning the Crusaders. They knew little, they cared less. There are a few historians who give the Crusades a passing mention. A man of genius like the early thirteenth-century historian Ibn al-Athir was even able to detect a connection between the reconquest in Spain and Sicily and the arrival of the Crusaders in the Levant. For a man of his time, writing in Iraq, that was a quite remarkable piece of historical vision. But this was an exception.

We should therefore not be surprised to find a lack of any kind of empathy with the outsider. Now empathy is not a strictly modern phenomenon. The prophet Jonah was reminded that the people of Nineveh were also people, that one should not delight in their defeat. The Greek dramatist Aeschylus shows compassion for the defeated Persians in a war in which he himself had been a combatant. In contrast, I have not come across anything of that kind in Muslim sources.

This lack of interest and empathy continues right into the Ottoman centuries. One is struck by the fact, for example, that the Thirty-Years War — an event that should have interested the Ottomans, raging as it did just beyond their frontiers — is mentioned in the contemporary Ottoman chronicle only in a very brief and error-ridden entry of a couple of pages. But interest in outside history finally begins, as one would expect, with the Ottomans, and it begins when the Ottomans were becoming aware that things were going wrong, that these picturesque barbarians beyond the frontier could actually be dangerous.

We then find attempts to write historical accounts of Europe, one from the seventeenth century, two or three from the eighteenth century. Efforts begin in earnest in the early nineteenth century, when the Ottomans could no longer be unaware of the looming danger that Europe represented to the very survival of Muslim independence in the central lands. We then see the first translations from Western languages into Arabic, Persian and Turkish. The choice of books for translation is telling. A very large proportion are biographies: Napoleon, Catherine the Great of Russia, Charles XII of Sweden, and one wonders why a historiographic tradition which never took to royal biography becomes so concerned with the royal biography of others.

The Ends of History-Writing

What then has been the function and the purpose of history in the Islamic world? Why did people pay historians to write the stuff, and to teach it? Three major purposes emerge.

The first is what one might call the didactic: one needs to study the past and to relate and explain what happened in the past so that we may learn from the past and teach others. This is, I think, the most basic and important purpose, and it is for this that Islam especially assigns a central religious importance to history and accuracy. Here one might mention the example of the Ottoman *vaqanüvis* — the imperial historiographer, a court official appointed by the sultan whose job it was to chronicle current events. What is striking about the Ottoman court chroniclers is their extraordinary frankness. Major defeats, like the battle of Lepanto and the failures to take Vienna, are described with devastating candor. I remember a phrase of Silihdar, a contemporary Ottoman historian of the second defeat of Vienna. He tells the story in picturesque detail and ends by saying: "This is the most crushing defeat suffered by the house of Osman since the foundation of our state." It is difficult to imagine a modern historian in most countries of the Middle East using that kind of language about a contemporary defeat.

A second purpose is what one might call the practical: one learns about what people did in the past in order to repeat their successes and avoid their errors. Hence, a number of Muslim historical writings have the word *i'bar* in the title or something to the same effect — examples to be followed.

A third purpose of the writing of history is to legitimize, justify, advertise, promote, persuade, and indoctrinate. In pre-modern times, this is surprisingly rare. Historians on the whole tell it like it was. Occasionally, when they don't, they confess. There are some striking passages in Tabari, for example, where he confesses in so many words to suppressing some information as not being in the public interest. For the most part, however, such suppression is a modern practice that arrives only with nationalism and nationalist historiography. Some years ago, the Turkish historian Halil Inalcik wrote an article on modern historical writing in the Middle East, and he quoted a Syrian government ministry of education circular on the teaching of history in schools. There it was stated that the purpose of teaching history in the schools is to strengthen national awareness and loyalty.[1] That, I think, is a very widely-held view, though it isn't usually expressed with such frankness, nor is it confined to Syria.

Yet even distant history must be controlled because of the extraordinary extent to which historical awareness is still alive among the mass of the people. I am not saying that their awareness of the past is necessarily an accurate one. History in the popular consciousness may be highly inaccurate, but nevertheless it is very powerful. If one looks at the political propaganda conducted by the two sides in the Iraq-Iran war, it is full of rapid and incomplete allusions to a remote past for which no explanation was necessary because the target audience understood. When the Iranian mullahs referred to Saddam Hussein as Yazid, everybody knew what they meant; there was no need for explanation. When the Iraqis spoke of the great victory of Qadisiyya, it was a bit more complicated because both sides claimed to be the victors of Qadisiyya. If it was a victory of Arabs over Persians, then the Iraqis could claim it; but if it was a victory of Muslims over infidels, then the Iranians could claim it. Not surprisingly, both did claim it, in an interesting example of the re-valorization of past events in modern terms. There are many other evocative names from early Islamic history. When an Egyptian military operation was given the name Badr, its meaning was clear; when negotiators refer to Hudaybiyya, again the context is well known, although the interpretations may vary. The control of historiography remains as important as ever, perhaps even more so with the spread of mass media.[2]

Whose History?

The question of the study of Islamic history is the last topic to which I shall refer. May we non-Muslims study it? Should we? And if the answer to both is yes, then how?

May we? Until a few years ago, it would not have occurred to anyone to ask the question. Now it is asked all the time, and it must be answered. There is a prevailing view, particularly in politically correct circles, that history is a national possession which belongs to the people who made it, and that others have no right to deal with it. We must let "them" — whatever that means — study "their" history, and be content with what they give to us for our edification. This is a point of view I find totally unacceptable. All that is human belongs to all of us, and I cannot see any justification, intellectual or other, for this kind of nationalized history. I derive great satisfaction from the fact that in my own university, Princeton, Talmud is taught by a Christian woman (which would seem to constitute not one but two strikes against her).

Should we? There are many people who ask why we should bother with these strange and exotic peoples. We have enough to do to learn our own history, which is all that really matters to us. Why go to the trouble? Again I think that we should bother; perhaps not all of us but certainly a lot of us. The history of Islam is a vital and essential part of human history without which even "our" own history is not fully intelligible.

And how? In a scholarly, meticulous, careful, precise way. No one can achieve complete freedom from bias. But as the American economist Robert Solo once remarked, while you cannot achieve complete asepsis, this is no reason to perform surgery in a sewer. We do the best we can. This means using the new sciences that have been created for the study of documents, inscriptions, coins, and the like, and trying to achieve a better understanding of the past through methods and sources not previously available.

The study of Islamic history in the Western world has gone through three phases. In the first, historians believed everything they were told. They read chronicles, were impressed by their detail, quantity, and manifest concern for accuracy, and so assumed that whatever they said was true. Then came a second phase, when the great nineteenth-century scholars began to apply critical method, treating Muslim historians in the same way they had treated Greek, Latin, and their own historians, trying to detect biases, distortions, variant versions and so on. Here I am thinking particularly of the work of such founding fathers of our discipline as de Goeje, Wellhausen, Caetani and others. Then more recently comes a third phase, of almost total rejection. It is all false, it is all invented; we know absolutely nothing.

From my presentation, you will have gathered that I do not hold that opinion. What we have to do now is to find a more balanced approach, critical but not destructive, which will enable us to achieve a better understanding of the human history we all share.

NOTES

1. Halil Inalcik, "Some Remarks on the Study of History in Islamic Countries," *Middle East Journal* , vol. 6 (1953): 551-55.
2. For other aspects of this issue, see Stephen Humphreys, "Modern Arab Historians and the Challenge of the Islamic Past," *Middle Eastern Lectures*, no. 1 (1995): 119-31. *Ed*.

The Commensality of Islamic and Jewish Civilizations

by Norman A. Stillman

Judaism and Islam, like Judaism and Christianity, have had a long intermeshed history. But the Judeo-Christian historical encounter began with the breakaway of a sect from within the Jewish fold, and developed early on into a fiercely competitive, highly inimical, and ultimately destructive relationship. In contrast, the Judeo-Muslim encounter, though not without its stresses and tensions, was marked from the very beginning and for long periods of time thereafter by cultural intercourse within a common civilizational context: Islamic civilization.

In this lecture, I shall be taking my Islamic civilizational framework much more broadly than the sociologist Marshall Hodgson, for whom civilization meant first and foremost a conscious sharing of "interdependent cumulative traditions...on the level of 'high culture'," reaching its summit "at the urban, literate level of complexity and sophistication."[1] While I agree with the importance of high culture as a criterion for identifying a civilization (and the first part of this lecture will focus on this aspect), I find this view much too narrow. For high culture rests upon a profound substratum of popular culture. The latter is not merely the substrate bedrock foundation of the former. It contains subterranean springs that well up into the high culture and intermingle with it.

I have often found that knowledge of popular culture facilitated my understanding and illuminated and clarified innumerable aspects in such eminently high culture areas as official religion, law, and literature. This goes both for the study of Judaism (not merely within the Islamicate context) and Islam. And I would hasten to add that knowledge of high culture, in turn, facilitates interpretation of popular culture. Because just as the one wells up, elements of the other percolate down. Due to this co-mingling, it is not always possible to isolate a discussion of Islamic and Jewish high culture from their popular counterpart.

It has become a commonplace to refer to the cultural interaction in history between Islam and Judaism and between Muslims and Jews by the biological metaphor of symbiosis, a term popularized by S. D. Goitein in his book *Jews and Arabs,* although the idea itself goes back to the *Wissenschaft des Judentums* scholars of the nineteenth century.[2] However, since symbiosis can be characterized either by a parasitic or commensal form of mutualism, I prefer to describe the interrelationship by the term commensality, which not only implies living together in a shared environment (like the Spanish term *convivencia,* often used by historians of medieval Iberia), but also, as its Latin root would indicate, "sharing from the same table" (in this case a table of culture, not comestibles).

The Beginnings of Judeo-Islamic Commensality

As is well known, the encounter between Judaism and Islam goes back to the very birth of the latter in Arabia in the seventh century. I do not wish to get involved here in what has become overall an arid and futile debate that began with Abraham Geiger in the last century and was followed in this one by Charles Torrey, Richard Bell, Tor Andrae and S. D. Goitein, as to who were the primary sources of inspiration for Muhammad's religious message. I would simply say that a considerable body of religious concepts, ethical notions, homiletic lore and scriptural topoi were disseminated among the pagan Arabs by Jews, Christians, and various sectarians, including, perhaps, Judeo-Christians and Gnostics.[3] Taking into account Julian Obermann's caveat that seemingly Jewish material could have come to Muhammad's attention from Christians and vice versa,[4] there is still much that is specifically and identifiably of Jewish origin in early Islam. A great body of extra-Qur'anic lore which comprises an important part of scriptural exegesis *(tafsir al-qur'an)* and prophetic hagiography *(qisas al-anbiya')* is actually called *isra'iliyyat,* or Israelite narratives.

But more significant than any borrowed or shared elements in Judaism and Islam are: 1) the attitude of Islam toward Judaism, Christianity and Zoroastrianism, and 2) the very structural model of Islam itself as a religion.

Islam's attitude toward Judaism is particularly significant, because it it provided the psychological framework for later commensality. Unlike Christianity, Islam did not begin as a sect within Judaism and did not claim to be Verus Israël, but merely the last and best of a series of divine revelations. There is nothing in either the Qur'an or later Muslim theological writings that is comparable to the overwhelming preoccupation with Jews and Judaism that one finds in the New Testament, Patristic literature and other Christian writings.

In the Islamic view, Jews shared the status of *ahl al-kitab* (scriptural people) with the far more numerous Christians and Zoroastrians. As long as they submitted to the suzerainty of the Islamic state, paid tribute, and comported themselves with the humble demeanor of subjects, they were entitled to the protection of the Muslim community, and hence their legal designation as *ahl al-dhimma* (protégés). Despite certain restrictions, they enjoyed freedom of cult (within discreet limits), freedom of economic endeavor, and a great measure of internal communal autonomy.

The second factor which helped to lay the groundwork for the later commensality was the structural model of Islam itself, which was far closer to that of Judaism than Christianity. Both Islam and Judaism share an uncompromising, iconoclastic monotheism. Both possess the notion of a religious polity governed by divine law. Thus, Islam was not perceived by Judaism as idolatrous *(avoda zara)* as Christianity was perceived. Indeed, when Islam burst upon the scene of history as the Arab armies poured out of the Arabian desert into the surrounding lands, Jewish apocalyptic literature depicted the conquests as a divine visitation upon wicked Edom, the code word for Byzantine Christendom.

The three hundred years following the Islamic conquests witnessed the transformation of much of world Jewry that now lived within the Dar al-Islam into an essentially urban population. The process whereby Jews went over from an agrarian way of life to a cosmopolitan one had begun in late antiquity, but was now completed in the wave of urbanism that occurred as a direct result of the conquests.[5]

This was also the period when Jews from Spain in the west to Iraq in the east went over to speaking Arabic, the lingua franca of the new *oikoumene.* But more important than merely adopting Arabic in speech, by the tenth century Jews were using Arabic for nearly all forms of written expression, including in the religious domain. Queries and responsa, scriptural exegesis, legal documents, and treatises of all sorts were written in Arabic, albeit normally in Hebrew characters. One reason for this thorough linguistic assimilation, as Joshua Blau has pointed out, is that in the Jewish heartlands of Palestine, Syria, and Iraq (Bavel), Arabic supplanted Aramaic, the previous lingua franca of both Jews and Gentiles. Aramaic had already been used for all purposes, religious and profane.

Therefore, the transition to Arabic seemed a natural process affecting everyone, irrespective of nationality or confession.

To this I would add three other reasons. First, there was the recognized familial kinship of Arabic to Aramaic — and of course to Hebrew — that mitigated against any feeling of foreignness. Second, there was the prestige of Arabic within Islamic society, a veritable cult of language, which did have its own psychological impact on Islamicate Jewry. Third, there was a secular aspect of general culture for which Arabic was the medium and that could be safely shared. By contrast, no such parallel existed in Christendom at the time, where Latin was the language of a thoroughly clerical culture and the vernaculars enjoyed no comparable prestige.

Commensality in High Culture in the Middle Ages

Judeo-Islamic commensality in the domain of high culture was most apparent during the ninth through thirteenth centuries. The initial environment for this intellectual and cultural mutualism was Iraq, which after the Abbasid revolution of 750 became the center of the Islamic world, but which, as Bavel, was already the center of the Jewish world since long before. In Iraq, the process of the formulation and development of Jewish and Islamic law occurred side by side, and indeed the very conception of an all-embracing religious law as "path" (Hebrew, *halakha*; Arabic, *shari'a*) in both cultures was parallel. Iraq/Babylonia, which was the site of the great talmudic academies that had been in existence for more than half a millennium when the Abbasid caliphate was established, now was the site of some of the early schools of Islamic law. The forerunner of the *madrasa* evolved in close geographical propinquity to the *bet midrash* and the *yeshiva/methivta*. In fact, in early usage, the Arabic *majlis* was a Muslim parallel to the Jewish *yeshiva/methivta*.

The many striking parallels between *halakha* and *shari'a* in their scope of application, formulation, and methodology, pose problems rather than solving them. As Goitein has noted, these similarities might be the product of parallel development rather than borrowing.[6] Conceivably by this time, similarities and parallels might well be due to Islamic influences upon Judaism no less than to Jewish influences on Islam. The question "who took what — if anything — from whom?" for the most part cannot be answered satisfactorily in our present state of knowledge. Furthermore, it is beside the point. What is the point is that Muslim and Jewish scholars operated in a similar universe of religious, legal, and intellectual discourse, shared similar concerns and attitudes, and were not unaware of what the others were doing.

The study of sacred law was the most Jewish and Muslim of cultural pursuits. Despite similarities and parallels, despite the common environment, they were clearly delineated by confessional boundaries. Cultural commensality was far greater, far more directly discernible, in other areas of high culture and in particular in those areas of scientific and intellectual endeavor that were a direct outgrowth of the medieval Hellenic revival which flowered in Iraq beginning in the ninth century.

The "Islamic Renaissance" — as Adam Mez once dubbed it — witnessed the absorption of much of the Hellenic corpus of science and philosophy through systematic translation into Arabic. The translators were primarily Syriac Christians, although one or two isolated Jewish individuals, such as Masarjawayh of Basra are known. Overall, the direction of cultural transmission is quite clear: Islamicate Jewry assimilated high culture from the broader Islamic society. Now this renascence of classical knowledge happened to coincide with the so-called "Commercial Revolution" and the rise of a Jewish bourgeoisie which, like its Muslim counterpart, was interested in secular intellectual pursuits. In the cosmopolitan urban environment of Baghdad and other cities, there was widespread interconfessional contact within intellectual society. The famous, somewhat shocked eyewitness description of intellectual gatherings in Baghdad by the tenth-century Andalusian theologian Ibn Sa'di, is but one of many accounts of nonsectarian cultural intercourse.

Within this intellectual environment, Jewish religious leaders followed their Muslim counterparts in adopting philosophy in the defense of religion, often to meet similar challenges raised by free-thinking heretics like Hiwi al-Balkhi in Judaism who raised the same rationalist challenges that men, such as Ibn al-Rawandi and Abu Bakr al-Razi, did in Islam. Jewish laymen, like Muslim laymen, were given over to "confusion" caused by competing claims to truth and the same seeming incompatibility of Greek science and revealed religious dogmas. (The very term for this "confusion," *shubha,* is used by both Sa'adya Gaon in his *Amanat wal-I'tiqadat* and by Qadi Abd al-Jabbar in his *al-Mughni.)* As every major student of Judeo-Arabic philosophy and theology has shown — from Munk in the nineteenth century to Guttmann and Wolfson in the twentieth — medieval Jewish philosophical thinking borrowed its language and methodology from the *kalam* theologians, particularly the Mu'tazila, and from the Islamic philosophers.

Jewish scholars at this time also adopted the Arab linguistic sciences of grammar and lexicography *(fiqh al-lughra)* which they applied to Hebrew for the new style of biblical exegesis pioneered by Sa'adya in the tenth century and which reached its apogee with Abraham Ibn Ezra in the eleventh-twelfth centuries. These three fields — grammar, lexicography, and scriptural exegesis — were cultivated by the Rabbanite community as a response to the threat of the Karaite schism within Judaism. The Karaites, it will be recalled, had already adopted these tools because of their rejection of Rabbinic Oral Tradition with its strong midrashic component and their insistence upon the biblical text as sole authority.

The pursuit of lingusitic studies eventually became an end in and of itself as Jews — especially in Spain — assimilated Islamic civilization's cult of language, albeit with Hebrew rather than Arabic as the object of national pride. It is for this reason that poetry — and remember, poetry was the ultimate art form in Islamic civilization — remained exclusively in Hebrew in Jewish high culture even when it had adopted Arabic meters and secular themes (and even when these themes were antithetical to Jewish values, as for example in the case of carousing and homosexuality). It is not (as Joshua Blau has suggested) that Jews did not possess the mastery of classical Arabic that the composition of Arabic poetry required. Some in fact did. Nor was it because (as Blau has also suggested) that the ideals of Bedouin society were alien to the sophisticated urban Jews. By this time, the ideals of the Arabian desert were alien to most of urban Muslim society as well. Besides, Jews did write poetry on such alien themes as the love of young boys. Rather, it was for the "nationalistic" reasons that I noted above that Hebrew was the exclusive medium for Jewish poetic expression.[7] Islamicate Jewry absorbed many aspects of the high culture of the "Renaissance of Islam." No less important, it assimilated its *mentalité et sensibilités*. It participated in and contributed to certain secular aspects of the cosmopolitan general culture that transcended confessional lines, notably in the domains of science and philosophy. But commensality on the level of high culture never meant total assimilation. This simply could not occur in a traditional, hierarchal society in which religion was the hallmark of individual identity, the ultimate goal of individual concern, and the determinant of individual social and political status.

The "Renaissance of Islam," combining material prosperity and strong, cosmopolitan, secular elements, had created a climate, a meeting ground, in which a Judeo-Islamic commensal symbiosis could take place on the level of high culture. From the mid-thirteenth century on, however, it was precisely these cosmopolitan, secular aspects of the high culture of classical Islamic civilization that were eclipsed, as the clerical, religious elements which had always been significant in Islamic civilization came to predominate. This social and intellectual transformation is frequently explained according to the model of decadence after efflorescence. However, it should be seen as an adaptation by Islamic civilization to historical challenges from within and without. These changes resulted in an environment that was no longer conducive to continued commensality in the domain of high culture. During this period of the later Islamic Middle Ages, Jews, along with Christians, not only declined in actual numbers, but became more marginal within the society and the economy.

Commensality in Popular Culture: Later Middle Ages to Modern Times

In spite of these radical changes, the Judeo-Islamic commensality remained strong on the level of popular culture.

One reason for this continuity was that despite the progressive marginalizing of non-Muslims and in many places their social isolation within ghetto-like quarters, Jews were never as separated from their Gentile neighbors physically, linguistically, or culturally, as were Jews in Christian Europe. A second important reason is that a considerable part of the substratum of popular culture in Islamic civilization had existed prior to the advent of Islam. It was a Mediterranean popular culture that merged with Irano-Central Asian popular culture at its eastern end and African popular culture at its southwestern extreme.

To be sure, there were local and regional variations in North Africa, Anatolia, Egypt and the Levant, the Arabian peninsula, and Iran. But an important part of this popular culture was there even before. No less important was that until the mass immigration of Sephardim in the fifteenth and sixteenth centuries, most of Islamicate Jewry constituted an indigenous, autochthonous population that perceived itself to be even more rooted than the Arab and Turkish inhabitants in most of these lands. Indeed, so this Jewry was perceived by the Muslim majority, as an element deeply rooted in the local popular culture.

Perhaps the most striking areas of commensality in the domain of popular culture are (of all things) in that area where boundaries are strictest on the high culture level, namely religion and pietist practice. This is really not so surprising as it might seem at first blush. Students of religious studies and anthropology take for granted the wide divergence between the official "Great Way" and the popular "Lesser Way."

A prime example of commensality in popular religion amongst Jews and Muslims is the widespread veneration of holy men and the developed cult of saints with organized pilgrimages to their shrines or tombs — this, despite the fact that scholarly orthodoxy and the classical sources in both Judaism and Islam disapprove of such practices. Early Islam in fact condemned Christians and Jews for saint cults. In a well known *hadith*, the Prophet Muhammad is quoted as saying: "God's curse upon the Jews and the Christians who have made the graves of their prophets into places of worship." This condemnation, which is repeated throughout the canonical collections, did not prove sufficient to stem the growth of such shrines among Muslims.[8]

Many of the practices associated with saints' shrines show strong parallels between the Jewish and Muslim versions with regard to the individual pilgrimage, called *ziyara* (visit) by both, and with regard to the annual organized pilgrimage celebration called *hillula* (Aramaic for wedding celebration) by Jews and *mawsim* (Arabic for seasonal time) by Muslims. Not only are many of the practices similar, but so is the very spatial organization of the pilgrimages sites as well. I am not talking here merely about the architecture of the shrines, but rather how people and activities are spatially arranged around the site during the pilgrimage.

The most outstanding example of cultural commensality in the area of saint veneration is the sharing of certain saints and shrines by both Muslim and Jews. This is perhaps not so surprising in the case of tombs or shrines connected with biblical personalities, such as the tomb of Ezekiel at al-Kifl in Iraq or the tomb of the Patriarchs in Hebron. Nor is it so surprising for the shrines of anonymous saints and spirits associated with sacred trees, groves, brooks, pools, rocks and grottos. These sites have been held sacred throughout the ages, long before the advent of Judaism or Islam. They are perceived as points of hierophany where the sacred bursts forth into the mundane plane. One can find countless parallel instances of holy sites throughout the world.

Where the sharing may seem surprising is in the case of shrines dedicated to a saint who is clearly identified as Jewish or Muslim. This can work in a variety of ways. For example, both groups have pilgrimages to the holy place but at different times. Or, the shrine is the preserve of only one group who has exclusive rights of guardianship, but individuals from the other community come in times of need. Examples of the latter is the shrine of Sidi Mehrez in Tunis and of Rabbi Amran Ibn Diwan at Wazzan in Morocco. Sometimes members of one religious community play an ancillary role at the other community's celebration, as Muslims do at the *hillula* of Rabbi Amran. Sometimes, of course, there is a dispute as to the identity of the saint (as in the case of the sacred grotto outside Sefrou, Morocco) or the ownership of the shrine (as has happened over the ages with Ezekiel's tomb at al-Kifl).[9]

Both Jews and Muslims in the Islamic world have hagiographic literature associated with saint veneration. By its very nature as a literate form, but due to its association with popular religion, this literature falls somewhere between high and popular culture. Both the Jewish and the Muslim hagiographic literature can be divided into three somewhat parallel sub-genres.

For Jews there are: 1) *shivhe zaddiqim* (praises of saints), 2) *ma'ase nissim* (miraculous seeds or *legenda d'ora)*, and 3) *hayye zaddiqim (vitae sanctorum)*. For Muslims the genres are: 1) *manaqib al-sadat* (virtues of saints), 2) *tabaqat ahl al-tasawwuf* (classes of Sufis), and 3) *tarajim* (biographical dictionaries). I must hasten to add here that despite some general parallels in the three categories, they seem to be little, if at all, influenced by each other. Each is deeply rooted in its respective literary traditions. The oral pious tales told about the saints by the non-literate population (or even by the semi-literate) would, I suspect, show greater affinities. However, I have not studied this systematically enough to go beyond impressions.[10]

This brief discussion of written and oral popular religious literature conveniently leads into another area of Judeo-Islamic commensality: general popular literature. This literature, which is both written and oral and includes both prose and poetry, has never been deemed to be literature by the high culture establishment among Jews or Muslims.

A prime example of this popular literature is narrative entertainment prose. In this case, the symbiosis was more parasitic than truly commensal. That is to say, the Jews were primarily consumers, but not producers of this genre. Jews did produce some entertainment literature of the high culture type during the ninth through thirteenth centuries, as for example Rabbi Nissim Ibn Shahin's *Kitab al-faraj ba'd al-shidda,* but even during this period when commensality in high culture was its apogee, we know that most Jews were not avid readers of Arabic belles lettres *(adab)* since they had their own belle lettristic tradition. We know from the Geniza lists of private library holdings (usually made for estate purposes) that works on science and philosophy comprised the majority of non-Jewish books in the homes of the Jewish intelligentsia. There were also works of popular entertainment literature in these personal libraries. The oldest known mention of the title *Alf layla wa-layla* (1001 Nights) comes in fact from the Geniza.[11] We also know from other evidence that Jews in the medieval Muslim world read Arabic popular literature. The twelfth-century Jewish apostate al-Samaw'al al-Maghribi informs us in the autobiographical introduction to his anti-Jewish polemic *Ifham al-Yahud* that as a teenager in Baghdad he loved to read the popular romances such as the Tales of Antar, Gests of Alexander, al-Battal, Dhu'l-Hima, and others.[12]

Entertaining stories of this sort, which by the way were read aloud in coffeehouses and other public places, were available in Judeo-Arabic versions up to modern times. With the advent of inexpensive printing in the nineteenth century, cheap penny handbooks in Judeo-Arabic gave this literature even wider circulation.

In addition to the high literary form of poetry, there has always existed a popular alter ego composed not in the classical language (the only recognized written medium), but in the vernacular. The only large body of medieval popular poetry which has survived in written form is the genre from Islamic Spain known as the *zajal.* The only other remains are isolated snippets cited by Arab authors. Much of this popular poetry (like popular prose for that matter) was not generally written down except in notebooks for performers who sang the poetry (or recited the stories). In Islamic Spain and later in the Maghrib, Jews were active in musical performance. Andalusian Jewish emigre musicians brought *zajal* notebooks *(zmayim* or *knanish)* to North Africa where they can still be found in library collections.

Just as Oriental Jews assimilated Islamic civilization's attitude toward poetry, so they also absorbed the concomitant love of music which in Arabic society borders on passion. Maimonides, by the way, who shared Plato's suspicion of music and the emotions it arouses, issued a responsum against the use of popular Arab amorous melodies in the synagogue service. The Rambam's disapproval notwithstanding, *paytanim* and *hazzanim* continued to employ not only the Arabic musical modes, but popular melodies for liturgical poetry. In the late nineteenth or early twentieth century, the chief rabbi of Alexandria, Elijah Bekhor Hazzan, knowing the place of music in Jewish society, ruled that it was permissible to hire Gentile musicians to play for Jewish family affairs held on Shabbat. This would be unthinkable in Ashkenazi orthodoxy.[13]

Outside of Jewish musician-singers who performed for Muslim audiences, most poetical compositions by Jewish men, the guardians of the literate high cultural tradition, continued to be in Hebrew up to modern times. Women, however, who generally did not know Hebrew, and often did not know to read or write even Judeo-Arabic, Ladino, or Judeo-Persian, as the case may be, did compose and transmit vernacular verse in all of its varied genres — wedding songs, love songs, satire, elegy — throughout the length and breadth of the Islamic world. In the Arabic-speaking world, which I have studied firsthand, many of these compositions by women are tied together with certain stock formulas, formulaic expressions and images in a process that is well known from orality research in other cultures.[14]

I want to mention just briefly one more genre of popular literary expression in which commensality is strongest, namely proverbs. Both Jews and Arabs had an ancient literary proverbial tradition. For the former, this tradition had its roots in the Bible and Rabbinic lore; for the latter, it was the Qur'an and *hadith,* but also pre-Islamic proverbs, collected in works such as Maydani's *Amthal al-Arab.* The vast majority of proverbs used in everyday life that have come down to modern times in the Arabic vernaculars are rarely from the classical Arabic literary tradition, but rather from the popular substratum of ancient Near Eastern wisdom literature. Although some proverbs are specifically Jewish or specifically Muslim, much of the proverbial genre that adds salt to daily speech belongs to a shared tradition of wit and wisdom.

The three examples of commensality on the level of popular culture that I have just elaborated — saint veneration, popular literature, and proverbs — are by no means isolated phenomena. Shared culture permeated daily life in all its aspects — for example, in the domain of material culture (food, clothing, living space, artisanry) and folk beliefs (evil eye, spirits, the use of amulets, traditional medicine). There were differences to be sure, some imposed by the dominant Muslim society, which required differentiation with regard to dress *(ghiyar)*. Other differences were self-imposed either consciously or subconsciously, as for example in the domain of language.[15]

The End of Judeo-Islamic Commensality?

One might think that the fourteen centuries of Judeo-Islamic commensality have come to an end. After all, the overwhelming majority of Islamicate Jews have left their lands of origin for Israel, France and elsewhere. Those who have stayed behind constitute for the most part a vestigial and moribund remnant. The adoption of new languages and cultural norms by the Jews who have emigrated from the Islamic world, the Arab-Israeli conflict, and the rise of what is referred to as Islamic fundamentalism, would all seem to mitigate against continued cultural commensality. Even before the mass exodus of Jews from the Muslim countries, the process of modernization was affecting Muslims and Jews very differently, causing social and cultural disorientation and reorientation for both groups. Bernard Lewis has even referred to "the end of the Judaeo-Islamic tradition."[16] But one should never, in the words of an old *bon mot,* predict anything, especially the future. With the resurgence of Oriental Jewish ethnicity in Israel in recent years, and even more recently and more significantly with the increased freedom of movement between Israel and Islamic countries, the total end of Judeo-Islamic commensality cannot be taken as a certainty.

NOTES

1. Marshall G. S. Hodgson, *The Venture of Islam: Conscience and History in a World Civilization*, vol. 1 (Chicago, 1974), p. 33.
2. S. D. Goitein, *Jews and Arabs: Their Contacts through the Ages* (New York, 1955; 3rd rev. ed., 1974). For a thoughtful recent discussion of the notion of Judeo-Islamic symbiosis, see Steven M. Wasserstrom, *Between Muslim and Jew: The Problem of Symbiosis under Early Islam* (Princeton, 1995), pp. 3-12 et passim.
3. Abraham Geiger, *Was hat Mohammed aus dem Judenthume aufgenommen?* (Baden, 1833); translated to English as *Judaism and Islam*, by F. M. Young (Madras, 1898; repr. ed. with a Prolegomenon by Moshe Pearlmann, New York,

1970); Charles Torrey, *The Jewish Foundation of Islam* (New York, 1933); Richard Bell, *The Origin of Islam in its Christian Environment* (London, 1926); Tor Andrae, *Der Ursprung des Islams und Christentum* (Uppsala and Stockholm, 1926); S. D. Goitein, "Who were Muhammad's Chief Teachers?," *Gotthold E. Weil Jubilee Volume* (Jerusalem, 1922), pp. 10-23 [Hebrew with English summary]; and idem, *Jews and Arabs*, pp. 50-61.

4. Julian Obermann, "Islamic Origins: A Study in Background and Foundation," *The Arab Heritage*, ed. Nabih Faris (Princeton, 1944), pp. 58-120.

5. Concerning this transition and its results, see Norman A. Stillman, "The Jew in the Medieval Islamic City," in *The Jews of Medieval Islam: Community, Society, and Identity*, ed. Daniel Frank (Leiden, 1995), pp. 3-13.

6. S. D. Goitein, "The Birth-Hour of Muslim Law," in his *Studies in Islamic History and Institutions* (Leiden, 1966), p. 126.

7. For a succinct summary of the parameters of this debate, see Joshua Blau, "Medieval Judeo-Arabic," in *Jewish Languages: Themes and Variations*, ed. Herbert H. Paper (Cambridge, Mass., 1978), pp. 121-31; and my "Response," in ibid., pp. 137-41.

8. Al-Bukhari, *Sahih*, "Salat," no. 48. For the many other instances of this *hadith*, see A. J. Wensinck et al., *Concordance et indices de la tradition musulmane*, tome 5 (Leiden, 1965), p. 230b, s.v. *qubur*. In some variants of this *hadith* only the Jews are mentioned. For the cult of holy men in Islam, see Ignaz Goldziher, "Veneration of Saints in Islam," in his *Muslim Studies*, ed. S. M. Stern and trans. C. R. Barber and S. M. Stern (London, 1971), pp. 255-341.

9. Shared pilgrimage sites in Morocco are the subject of a book by Louis Voinot, *Pèlerinages judéo-musulmans du Maroc* (Paris, 1948). Voinot's list of more than one hundred sites is augmented several fold by Issachar Ben-Ami, *Saint Veneration among the Jews in Morocco* (Jerusalem, 1984) [in Hebrew]. Concerning the dispute over the identity of the saints of the Sefrou cave, see Norman A. Stillman, *The Language and Culture of the Jews of Sefrou, Morocco: An Ethnolinguistic Study* (Manchester, 1988), pp. 89-90, n. 5. Concerning the dispute over the ownership of Ezekiel's tomb which became a subject of international diplomatic intervention in the nineteenth century, see Norman A. Stillman, *The Jews of Arab Lands in Modern Times* (Philadelphia, 1991), pp. 389-92.

10. For a more detailed discussion, see Norman A. Stillman, "Saddiq and Marabout in Morocco," in *The Sepharadi and Oriental Jewish Heritage: Studies*, ed. Issachar Ben-Ami (Jerusalem, 1982), pp. 489-500.

11. The *Fihrist* of Ibn al-Nadim (d. 895) mentions an earlier incarnation of this work, the *Hezar Efsane*, or 1000 Tales.

12. Translated in Stillman, *The Jews of Arab Lands*, p. 230.

13. Concerning this remarkable individual, see Norman A. Stillman, *Sephardi Religious Responses to Modernity* (United Kingdom, United States: Harwood Academic Publishers, 1995), pp. 29-47.
14. The classic study of oral poetic composition is Albert B. Lord, *The Singer of Tales* (Cambridge, Mass., 1960). For an example of one Jewish woman's oral poetry, see Norman A. Stillman and Yedida K. Stillman, "The Art of a Moroccan Folk Poetess," *Zeitschrift der Deutschen Morgenländischen Gesellschaft*, vol. 128, no. 1 (1978): 65-89.
15. For thoughts on the process of linguistic differentiation, see Norman A. Stillman, "Contacts and Boundaries in the Domain of Language: The Case of Sefriwi Judeo-Arabic," in *Jews among Arabs: Contacts and Boundaries*, ed. Mark R. Cohen and Abraham L. Udovitch (Princeton, 1989), pp. 97-111; and idem, "Language Patterns in Islamic and Judaic Societies," in *Islam and Judaism: 1400 Years of Shared Values*, ed. Steven M. Wasserstrom (Portland, Oregon, 1991), pp. 41-55.
16. Norman A. Stillman, "Middle Eastern and North African Jewries Confront Modernity: Orientation, Disorientation, Reorientation," in *Sephardi and Middle Eastern Jewries: History and Culture in the Modern Era*, ed. Harvey E. Goldberg (Bloomington and Indianapolis, 1996), pp. 59-72; Bernard Lewis, *The Jews of Islam* (Princeton, 1984), pp. 154-91.

Patriotism and Faith:
Giorgio Levi Della Vida

by Dan V. Segre

I am neither a historian nor an orientalist, and therefore I am doubly honored to participate in this gathering of friends and admirers of Bernard Lewis, deliberating on the theme of "The Jewish Discovery of Islam." But I suspect that I have been asked to speak on Giorgio Levi Della Vida for two reasons.

The first is that, even after almost sixty years of life in Israel, I am still considered an Italian. The second is that I am old enough to have met Giorgio Levi Della Vida in 1949, when I served as an attaché at the Israeli legation in Rome. I called on him at his home in Via Po 33, where part of his family still resides, to ask his opinion on the chances of the Rhodes armistice agreements turning into permanent peace — a possibility which he rightly regarded as remote. But I also wanted to meet one of the three Italian Jewish professors who gave up university chairs in 1931 rather than register in the Fascist party. In all of Italy, only twelve lecturers (out of 1,225 university teachers) gave up their academic positions rather than join the Fascist party. At the time, Mussolini's behavior was quite moderate, and most of the other Jewish professors, Attilio Momigliano among them, supported Fascism, as did the majority of Italian Jews.

My impression is that Giorgio Levi Della Vida did not become an anti-Fascist or an Islamicist because he was a Jew. He became both as an Italian, as one of those totally assimilated Italian Jews vaguely proud of their origins, who had broken away from their ancestors' traditions and developed a humanistic, universal approach to religion and politics, feeling in a way more Italian than the Italians. The Jews of Italy, wrote Gramsci, were the only Jews in Europe who, with the Venetians, Napolitans, and Romans, were equal co-founders of a new national identity.

There was also nothing particularly Jewish in Levi Della Vida's decision to enter the field of oriental studies. His original vocation was in fact ancient Greek and Latin. What diverted his interest was love — or rather, unrequited love.

In a delightful book of memoirs, *Fantasmi Ritrovati* (Ghosts Recovered), published in 1966, there is a vague reference to this love in the form of a sonnet he wrote to a girl when he was twenty. She was the beautiful daughter of the first and only Jewish mayor of Rome, Ernesto Nathan, an Italian politician born in England, twice grand master of Italian Freemasons and a devoted friend of Giuseppe Mazzini, who died in his house. Levi Della Vida's disappointment was made harder to bear by the fact that the young lady in question married his own brother. To overcome his grief, he left for Egypt, and his interest in the East became his life's passion.

Born in Venice in 1886, the third son of Ettore Levi Della Vida, Giorgio belonged to a mixed Italian Sephardi family of Jewish intellectuals and patriots. That particular group of Levis came from Ferrara and they merged with the Della Vida, who had come from Spain, where a street near the cathedral of Seville still bears their name. "For two generations," writes Levi Della Vida,

> my family had detached itself from the practice of the Jewish religion. Brought up without any religious indoctrination, supposedly substituted by the vague theism of my mother and by the religion of duty and humanism of my father, one day I found within and around myself a great void which needed to be filled. Two ways were open to me: to return to the ancestral faith, of which I perceived the august majesty and which my family had put aside without formally denying it, or the resolute entry into the fold of the Catholic Church, which attracted me by its harmonious and solid doctrinal structure and by the very strong emotional charge of its cult.

From the intensive reading, when still a *liceum* student, of the lives of Jesus written by Holbach, David Friedrich Strauss and Ernest Renan, "I developed the interest in the studies of Semitic philology which became my profession, while I never made the choice (that this reading) should have caused." This early interest in Christianity acquainted him with some leading Church personalities of his time, among them the famous preacher and later supporter of Fascism, Father Giovanni Semeria, and Don Giovanni Genocchi, who was a very powerful figure, missionary and oriental scholar. These friendships drew Della Vida as a curious outsider (a chapter of his memoirs is significantly called "A Jew Among Modernists") into the violent debate for and against modernism which raged in Italy within and without the Catholic Church at the turn of the nineteenth century.

He joined the fight with a short article published in 1909 in the Roman journal *La Cultura,* entitled "New Theology, Modernism and Orthodoxy." This article would not be relevant to this lecture had it not been part of an intellectual and emotional debate which Levi Della Vida carried on with himself throughout his life. To a reader of his memoirs it reveals the intimate, unachieved vocation of the mystic.

"The mystic is a person," Levi Della Vida wrote in that article, "in whom coexist often without reciprocal interference two diametrically opposed tendencies: its effusion in the union with divine essence and rational, controlled behavior when dealing with earthly matters." Levi Della Vida never allowed these two tendencies to combine, and that was the source of the doubts which seem to have tormented him to the very last day of his life. In spite of this, or perhaps thanks to it, he was able to look at religion with the detached sympathy of the historian, and at history with the empathy of the truly religious man. It was this constant element in his works on the Semites — Jews and non-Jews — on which I would like to dwell, before concluding with some of his reflections on more contemporary problems of Middle East politics on which he wrote extensively.

The Making of a Scholar

In Rome, if you stand in front of Venezia Square, facing the famous balcony from which Mussolini harangued to the crowds, on your left, along the wall of Palazzo Venezia, runs a large street called Botteghe Oscure (Dark Shops). For the last half century, this street has been associated with the Italian Communist Party as the Quai d'Orsay is associated with the French foreign ministry. But in 1908, when Levi Della Vida returned from his first trip to Egypt, the street was far less famous except for the fact the Prince of Teano, Leone Caetani, lived there and turned the attic of his palace into a private center for oriental studies.

The prince was an amateur of great scholarship, an enchanting and at the same time pathetic figure, of whom Levi Della Vida has left us a vivid portrait in his memoirs. Della Vida was invited to join a small group of young researchers "full of enthusiasm and with empty pockets" in this aristocratic attic, to help the prince in his ambitious and never-completed enterprise, the *Annali dell'Islam,* a massive project of translating ancient Arab texts.

Levi Della Vida did not spend many years under the patronage of the prince, but in the Caetani mansion and its splendid library he prepared himself to compete successfully for the chair of Arabic at the Oriental Institute of Naples in 1914, at the age of twenty-eight. It was the first academic step along the road which led him to replace, in 1920, his teacher, the renowned orientalist Ignazio Guidi, in the chair of Hebrew and comparative Semitic languages in Rome — a chair dating from the fourteenth century for the study of holy scriptures in their original languages.

At the same time, and for a short period, his scientific activities were supplemented by political ones, expressed in many articles. In 1925 he signed the manifesto of the intellectuals against Mussolini and became a leading member of an organization called the National Union, which was banned by Mussolini in 1926. For his stand he was both resented and respected by Giovanni Gentile, the Fascist minister of culture, a scholar and a philosopher who protected many anti-Fascist intellectuals, Jews and non-Jews. Gentile, assassinated in Rome in 1944, was an outstanding and tragic figure of Fascism. He never shared the implicit and later explicit anti-Semitism of the party, and he recognized the importance of Zionism, sending a message of congratulations to the Hebrew University on the occasion of its establishment. He also intervened with the Nazis in favor of many Jewish scholars in Germany.

More important and notable than Levi Della Vida's anti-Fascist endeavors was his revolutionary contribution to the study of Semitic civilizations. In the early part of the nineteenth century, this discipline, like other branches of humanistic knowledge, tended to play down the religious factors in favor of the economic and social ones. Levi Della Vida was one of the first to challenge this approach. He believed in an autonomous science of Islam, based on the study of the *shari'a*, the literary texts and the great philosophical systems of the Orient. He accused the orientalists of too rigid an attachment to the principle of *purus grammaticus.* These scholars "do not see nor hear anything outside the closed and arid field of their erudite researches." The study of oriental civilizations could not, of course, be carried out without knowledge of oriental languages. "A neglected philology," he wrote, "always takes its revenge." But in all his academic and journalistic writings, he took an anti-positivist position, placing the religious element next to the rationalist one. For him, the two elements formed a dualism, and they denied "the possibility of giving definite answers either to the questions of history or to the mystery of the unknown."

Spirituality, independent from any type of religious framework, remained Levi Della Vida's life quest, a quest in which his researches on Judaism occupied an important place. His first scientific article, written while still a university student, dates from 1907 and is entitled "Hebrew and Jewish Literature." It was followed in 1924 by his "Sacred and Profane History of Israel," "The Development of the Idea of God in Ancient Israel," "Judaism and Christianity," and his classic and much-discussed entry on the Jews in the *Enciclopedia Italiana,* as well as a small volume on the Jews for the use of secondary schools.

In all these works — as in those dealing with Islam — his fundamental credo emerges. "Historical science," he writes, "whenever honestly professed, does not put itself at the service of any party. A purely historical conception of the religion of Israel implies a world vision different from that of Christianity but also from any other positive religion. Such a conception does not put itself *against* but only outside religion."

Levi Della Vida's interest in Judaism was only a part of his orientalist vocation. I do not feel competent to deal with this aspect of his work. I shall only recall that it covered the gamut, from Syriac to Phoenician and Punic studies, from the tale of "An Egyptian in Granada in the Fifteenth Century" to the tale of "A Portuguese in Mecca in the Sixteenth Century." His last volume of Arab-Islamic studies, published in 1967, dealt with the pre-Islamic poetry of Arabia. It was in a sense the end of a road which started in 1915 with his long article on *Kitab ansab al-ashraf* of Baladhuri, and continued with his series on Arab-Islamic manuscripts from the Vatican Library which he published in 1935. The death of his wife in 1955, combined with a protracted period of ill-health, forced him to stop teaching. He continued to work at home and at the Vatican Library, and in 1965 published a last volume listing these manuscripts.

I would like to conclude this unscholarly excursion into his prodigious scientific work by mentioning two articles which are nearer to my journalistic interests. They are part of a collection entitled *Aneddoti e svaghi arabi e non arabi* (Arab and Non-Arab Anecdotes and Amusements), published in Milan in 1959.

The first is called "The Arabia of Lawrence." When Levi Della Vida first came across *The Revolt in the Desert* in 1930, he sent a copy of his review article to the man he called "the prince of the Islamicists," the Dutch professor Christiaan Snouck Hurgronje. Back came the answer in French, dated 6 October 1931. "How could you praise," wrote the famous Dutch professor, "even as an artist, such a despicable person, a sportsman who, thanks to millions of wasted pounds, succeeded in gathering around himself and the ambitious Faysal some tribes of bandits in whom he excited the worst instincts, and who has left no trace of his endeavors? Woe to the country which sees itself delivered to the whims of such an intellectual adventurer." Here is Levi Della Vida's response: "The mystery of Lawrence is not in his external but in his intimate life. This improvised officer reveals himself as a strategist in a grand style. The archaeologist of the ancient Orient plays masterfully with the politics of the modern Orient. But unfortunately for a few Arabists, the book has not been written for them. It has been written for tens of thousands of readers who happen to be sensitive to the magic of art."

The second article, entitled "Arab Nations and Arab Nationalism," was published in 1956. It was prophetic then and remains topical now. "The Arab nationalist faith is fundamentally nothing else but the repercussion and partly the conscious imitation of the Western nationalist phase," wrote Levi Della Vida. "After the First World War, when the new Arab states were beginning to consolidate themselves along the lines of the principle of nationality rooted in the idea of liberty, dictatorship replaced democracy in part of Europe, and nationalism stood to nationality as satanism stands to religion." He continued by saying that in the Arab states, totalitarian nationalism, helped by Fascist and Nazi propaganda, penetrated easily into fragile democratic structures. "It met and intermingled with Muslim fanaticism, which ignored (and was not alone in doing so) the fundamental anti-religious tendency (of totalitarianism), welcoming it as the enemy of secular democracies." The terrorist association of the Muslim Brotherhood, says Levi Della Vida, was the typical expression of this "national-Islamism." "One can laugh at Nasser's maximalist program," he wrote,

> when the industrial efficiency of fifty million Arabs is inferior to that of Switzerland... But if the dream itself is chimeric, the fact of its being dreamt represents a danger. The Arabs are without doubt a nation. They are rightly proud of their great past and of their more recent stupendous revival.... But if under the flag of national solidarity they should develop a destructive nationalistic spirit, this would constitute a danger for the peace and freedom of the world. It would become a malignant

tumor which, in the very name of peace and freedom, the common heritage of all nations, must be fought against and extirpated.

Unfinished Quest

When Levi Della Vida died in November 1967, at the age of seventy-nine, *The Times* wrote that the world of culture had lost "the greatest and the most honoured Italian orientalist... one of the most profound men and scholars of our generation." The academic recognition he obtained during his lifetime was impressive. He was made a member of the Institute of France, where he taught in 1938, as well as of the British, Belgian, Polish, and many other national academies. He received honorary doctorates from the universities of Paris, Algiers, and Jerusalem. The University of California gave his name and put his effigy on the medal periodically conferred on the best Islamic scholars. He was considered a mentor by many renowned Italian and non-Italian orientalists, historians, and archaeologists.

"The greatness of Levi Della Vida," wrote one of his most illustrious students, Sabatino Moscati, "is found in his exceptional capacity for synthesis, in the crystal clear representation of his idea. On the other hand, it comes out in the subtlety of his analytical notations, in the myriad of new ideas expressed even in short articles or just footnotes." Others compared Levi Della Vida to Sanchez-Albornoz and Menendez-Pidal, the great representatives of philological historiography, and to Gershom Scholem, for his ability to move from small details of the manuscript to the greater synthetic vision of the ideas and historical processes.

Yet the accolades never comforted Levi Della Vida. What deeply impressed me when going through some of his writing in preparation for this talk, was a letter which Levi Della Vida wrote to the French archaeologist Pierre Cintas in May 1966, describing how he felt after being made doctor *honoris causa* by the University of Algiers ten years before. "I was hit by a strong psychic depression upon my return from North Africa. Was it the realization of my lack of scientific preparation and of the miserable results of my activities? Was it the feeling of shame for the honors I received and which I felt totally unmerited? It was all this and many other reasons." The reasons, I dare say, were the honesty, intellectual integrity, civil courage and humility of a tormented religious conscience.

One might also discern the desire of a great scholar to send a message to all of us who deal with liberal arts. We spend time and effort trying to make sense of history, to understand human behavior, to interpret culture. When we compare the result of our efforts with those of the natural sciences, we cannot avoid questioning the value and the durability of our work. It is Levi Della Vida's constant questioning that makes his contribution so lasting, giving luster to the recognition it so rightly deserves.

ACKNOWLEDGEMENT

I am deeply grateful to Valeria Fiorani Piacentini, Levi Della Vida's niece and a distinguished professor of Islamic history and civilization at the Catholic University of Milan.

Occasions

Timur Kuran is Professor of Economics and the King Faisal Professor of Islamic Thought and Culture at the University of Southern California. He delivered the Thirteenth Annual Georges A. Kaller Lecture on 30 May 1996.

Bernard Lewis is the Cleveland E. Dodge Professor of Near Eastern Studies Emeritus at Princeton University. He delivered his lecture under the auspices of the Mortimer and Raymond Sackler Institute of Advanced Studies at Tel Aviv University, on 16 January 1995.

Judith Miller is a senior writer at *The New York Times*. She delivered her lecture at a conference entitled "Between Jihad and Peace: Islamist Alignments in a Changing Middle East," on 31 March 1996.

Yezid Sayigh is assistant director of the Centre of International Studies at Cambridge University. He delivered the Fourteenth Annual Joseph (Buddy) Strelitz Lecture on 12 December 1994.

Dan V. Segre is Professor of Political Science Emeritus at Haifa University. He delivered his lecture at a conference on "The Jewish Discovery of Islam," held in honor of Bernard Lewis's eightieth birthday, on 13 June 1996.

Norman A. Stillman is the Schusterman/Josey Professor of Judaic Studies at the University of Oklahoma. He delivered the Kalman Lassner Memorial Lecture on 5 June 1995.

Charles Tripp is Senior Lecturer in Politics at the School of Oriental and African Studies, University of London. His lecture was delivered on 26 April 1995, as the Twelfth Annual Georges A. Kaller Lecture.

P.J. Vatikiotis is Professor in Politics Emeritus at the School of Oriental and African Studies, University of London. He offered this summation at a conference on "Islam, Monarchy and Modernity in the Middle East," on 14 December 1995.

Recent Publications of the Moshe Dayan Center

The Middle East Contemporary Survey, volume 18, 1994, edited by Ami Ayalon and Bruce Maddy-Weitzman, published by Westview Press, 1996. 756 pp., $94.85 cloth.
> *The latest volume in the series that has become the standard reference work on Middle Eastern politics. Coverage now extended to the Maghrib.*

Arab Awakening and Islamic Revival: The Politics of Ideas in the Middle East, by Martin Kramer, published by Transaction Publishers, 1996. 297 pp., $34.95 cloth.
> *A collection of thought-provoking essays on the vicissitudes of Arabism and Islamism.*

Arab Politics in Israel at a Crossroads, edited by Elie Rekhess, published as Occasional Paper Number 119, by the Moshe Dayan Center, 102 pp., $9.95
> *Contributions by leading Israeli scholars and commentators, both Jews and Arabs.*

Newspapers and Periodicals of Jordan in the Press Archive of the Moshe Dayan Center, published by the Moshe Dayan Center, 47 pp., $6.00 paper.
> *First in a new series of country catalogues, with details on over 200 Jordanian publications in the Press Archive.*

The Press in the Arab Middle East: A History, by Ami Ayalon, published by Oxford University Press, 1995. 300 pp., $59.00 cloth.
> *The evolution of Arabic journalism from the 19th century through the Second World War, examining its political, social, and cultural roles.*

The Hashemites in the Modern Arab World: Essays in Honour of the late Professor Uriel Dann, edited by Asher Susser and Aryeh Shmuelevitz, published by Frank Cass, 1995. 264 pp., $40.00 cloth.
> *From the Arab Revolt of 1916 through the ill-fated Hashemite monarchy in Iraq and the present-day Kingdom of Jordan, colleagues of the late Uriel Dann look at a century of Hashemite history.*

Middle Eastern Lectures, Number One, edited by Martin Kramer, published by the Moshe Dayan Center, 1995, reprinted 1996. 133 pp., $12.95 paper.
> *Outstanding lectures by eight visitors to the Moshe Dayan Center, on themes ranging from the Palestine Mandate to Islam and democracy, from Turabi to the crisis of the Iranian revolution.*

Forthcoming

The Islamism Debate, edited by Martin Kramer, to be published as Dayan Center Paper Number 120 by the Moshe Dayan Center, ca. 160 pp., $12.95.
> *Contributions by nine scholars on the debate surrounding political Islam.*

To order, contact named publisher directly or send check payable to the Moshe Dayan Center to Publications Department, The Moshe Dayan Center, Gilman Building, Tel Aviv University, Ramat Aviv, Tel Aviv 69978, Israel. For foreign orders please add $1.00 per publication for surface postage and handling. For a full listing of all publications, please request our latest catalogue.